On Wings like Eagles

On Wings like Eagles

A Story of Faith, Forgiveness,
and Finding the Strength to Endure

Thomas Gregory Stewart

REDEMPTION PRESS

Published by Redemption Press, PO Box 427, Enumclaw, WA 98022.
Toll-Free (844) 2REDEEM (273-3336)

Redemption Press is honored to present this title in partnership with the author. The views expressed or implied in this work are those of the author. Redemption Press provides our imprint seal representing design excellence, creative content, and high-quality production.

The author has tried to recreate events, locales, and conversations from memories of them. In order to maintain their anonymity, in some instances the names of individuals, some identifying characteristics, and some details may have been changed, such as physical properties, occupations, and places of residence.

ISBN 13: 978-1-64645-363-4 (Paperback)
978-1-64645-362-7(ePub)
978-1-64645-364-1 (Mobi)

Library of Congress Catalog Card Number: 2016960858

DEDICATION

This book is dedicated to my late son, Benjamin Thomas Stewart. His death was the catalyst for understanding God's ultimate purpose for me. I love you, Benny! Fly, my son, soar high.

You intended to harm me, but God intended it for good to accomplish what is now being done, the saving of many lives.
—Genesis 50:20

CONTENTS

Foreword

By Dean Eric Smith

Everyone has a story. My story is that I forgave and helped save the life of the man that murdered my mother. After my journey was made into an award-winning documentary entitled, *Live To Forgive*, I had the opportunity to help people everywhere learn to forgive everyone for everything.

Since then, I've heard thousands of personal stories of forgiveness. Tom's incredible story is one of them.

Tom approached me during the lunch break of a full-day forgiveness seminar I was leading. After telling me about just a portion of the challenges God had helped him overcome, I said, "Oh my goodness, your story is like a movie."

We made plans to meet the next week for breakfast. This would be the first of dozens of meetings and the birth of a new friendship over the next decade. It was during these early morning meetings that Tom unveiled his riveting life story.

I wish everyone could have the pleasure of sitting at breakfast with the author of this book. I realize that's not possible, so allow me to share my experiences. What you'd discover is a humble and grateful man deeply committed to his faith and the task of spreading good news to those who will listen.

A few years into our friendship, I had the opportunity to help Tom prepare and present his testimony for the very first time at a men's breakfast at a local church. Each man in attendance was absolutely rocked by hearing just a fraction of what you're about to read. And

I mean, *rocked!* This was evidence that Tom's story needed to be shared with the world.

Many people have shared their stories of breakthrough, but few have had to convince others to believe it's even true in the first place. Tom persevered though—at great risk to himself. Tom's brave actions exposed a decades long, national cover-up that eventually upended one of the largest youth organizations in the country.

Life throws us a lot of curveballs. Tom knows that as much as anyone. His story proves that no matter what you've been through, if you keep your heart and mind fixed on Jesus, you will be personally restored and something good can come from your experience.

It's comforting to know that people like Tom, who have experienced such pain and despair, are living proof that this Scripture is true: "And we know that God causes everything to work together for the good of those who love God and are called according to his purpose for them" (Romans 8:28 NLT).

As Tom demonstrates in this book, there are two different dimensions of courage. One is the courage to face your challenges head-on. The second, and less talked-about dimension, is the unique ability to share what you've been through with others in hopes of helping them too.

Tom made the courageous decision to engrave his most challenging life experiences on his heart so that he can utilize them to help others who may be struggling with something similar. He's now uniquely qualified to encourage and inspire people who've gone through even the gravest of circumstances.

This is a rare book where you'll find yourself vacillating from one emotion to the next. Inspiration to suspense. Laughter to sadness. Hopelessness to hope.

In the end, you'll be riveted by the writing, captivated by the storytelling, and invigorated with new hope that you too, with Christ's help, can do all things.

Chapter 1

Looking for Belonging

BRUCE WAS SIXTEEN WHEN I met him. I was six. He lived with his parents in the white daylight rambler with a one-car garage at the end of my street, just left of the street sign at Dash Point Boulevard. I was practicing triple-play jump shots at the basketball court on our street with my younger brother, Matt, and best friend, Virgil, the day he strolled up.

"Mind if I join?" he asked.

Virgil tossed him the ball. "Sure. Now we can play two-on-two."

We paired up, each team with one younger boy and one older. Virgil was eight years older than me, and Bruce ten, so it was only fair. Besides, I didn't want to be on a team with my pesky younger sibling.

Bruce pushed his glasses up his nose, slicked back his plain brown hair, and started toward the basket. He was surprisingly quick given the extra pounds he carried on his frame. Bruce passed the ball to Matt, and I darted in front of him, blocking his attempt at a shot before stealing the ball.

"Tom, over here!" Virgil called.

I made a clean pass, and Virgil took a jump shot, swishing the net.

"Yes!" I threw my hands up in celebration. "Take that, Matt."

"Yeah, whatever," he shot back, swatting my hands down. Even though I was two years older than Matt, he was nearly as tall—and always out to beat me.

Virgil jogged over to give me a high five, his long hair blowing in the breeze. *Maybe Mother will let me grow my hair out too.* Virgil may

13

have been older, but he was a lonely outcast like me, and we'd become inseparable. With Dad gone working so much of the time, Virgil filled the void. And now I had another new friend—Bruce. I felt real cool having two older guys wanting to hang out with me.

A voice blared from a megaphone down the street, the amplified sound bouncing off the backboard of the hoop. "Where are you?" the voice called.

Bruce stopped dribbling the ball. "What was that?"

I sighed. "Our mother."

Screeching into the megaphone was Mother's sundown routine. She wasn't calling for dinner because Mother rarely cooked—maybe once a week. Most meals came from a mile-high stack of Swanson's TV dinners. When we'd all grown tired of food from foil tins, it was either takeout or whatever restaurant might still be open at 8:30 p.m. No, Mother just wanted to portray to the neighbors that she had concern for our whereabouts. The megaphone was our five-minute warning call to come home. If we didn't report for duty within five minutes, she'd lock the door—no exceptions.

Matt turned toward home with sluggish steps. "You coming?" he asked over his shoulder.

I stood still on the asphalt, weighing my decision. Pretending I didn't hear Mother had resulted in several sleepovers on Virgil's living room floor, which was a much better option than going back to lock-down with Sergeant Stewart on duty.

It was common knowledge in the neighborhood that my parents lacked certain qualities. Maybe that's why Virgil's mom, Mrs. Hess, always welcomed me with open arms. She appreciated my friendship with her son and offered safe haven from the troubles at home. Virgil had what I longed to have—a clean, happy home and a mother who loved him just as he was. Plus, Virgil's mom cooked regular meals. My cravings for home-cooked food often lured me over to the Hess's house right about when a normal dinner time would be. My stomach rumbled.

"You go ahead," I called after Matt.

Virgil's it is.

⁓✦⊙

Basketball tournaments with Bruce became a regular occurrence. There wasn't much to do in our small town of Dash Point, Washington. Located south of Puget Sound, it didn't even have its own city center, so we had to go across the bay to Tacoma. We played even when it rained, which was most of the year. One day, Bruce arrived decked out in his Boy Scout uniform. With a sash full of merit badges, he looked sharp—like a soldier in a military uniform. Bruce had recently achieved Eagle Scout, the highest ranking possible in the program. I was impressed, and from that moment, I decided I wanted to be a Scout too.

"How do I join?" I asked Bruce as he showed me each of his badges and explained how he'd earned them. He gave me a flyer to take home. Since I was seven, I was eligible to join Cub Scouts. Joining seemed like an opportunity to feel and act like a normal kid—somewhere I could belong.

That night, I waited impatiently for Dad to get home from work so I could show him the flyer. Dad had been an Eagle Scout too, and I hoped he would do Scouts with me. The lock clicked in the front door. Dad didn't see me at first. He hung up his keys and shrugged out of his jacket, then called down the hall, "Betty Lou, I'm home." No answer. He rubbed the weariness from his eyes, walked into the living room, and collapsed into his armchair. "Oh, hey, Tommy," he said, spotting me. I bounced over to him, flyer in hand.

"Dad, Bruce had the coolest uniform today, and he showed me his badges and told me about Cub Scouts, and it starts soon and—."

Dad raised a hand. "Whoa, slow down there and let me take a look." He glanced over the flyer, a pleased look spreading into his eyes. "So, you want to join Cub Scouts? This brings back memories." Dad looked over at me as if taking my measure. "Are you ready to take on this responsibility?"

"Yes, Dad, more than anything ever in my whole entire life!" I said, hardly able to contain my excitement. I wanted to feel important and mature, especially in Bruce's eyes. I was happy Dad seemed interested.

"What's this I hear?" Mother said, coming into the room. She brushed a strand of blond hair behind her ear and snatched up the flyer.

"Please, Mother, can I do it?" I asked. Mother's slight frame housed a strong-willed Norwegian, and I never knew how she would react.

Mother paused, her blue eyes narrowing, then passed the flyer back to Dad. "Well, you had better go into this at full speed and with flying colors, Tommy, or not at all. And it had better not interfere with your schoolwork, sports, and church." She turned to Dad. "Bob, you're late."

They began quarreling, but I tuned it out. I was already picturing becoming an Eagle Scout.

Becoming
a Boy Scout

THE FIRST PACK MEETING WAS scheduled for October 6—my eighth birthday. Since Matt's birthday was also in October, Mother usually combined them and split the difference for one celebration. I didn't think it was fair to either of us. At least having my first Cub Scout meeting on my birthday made the day more special.

That afternoon after school, I tried on my new uniform for the first time, relieved to be free from the matching Stewart plaids or those glowing orange terry cloth socks Mother always made us wear. It was nice not to have to rummage through my dirty clothes hamper to find something clean. Mother despised doing laundry, and I rarely had clean clothes. Lucky for me, a clean and pressed uniform was mandatory for each meeting.

Bruce arrived promptly at 6:15 p.m. to pick me up. Dad had volunteered to be my Cubmaster, but he had to rush straight to the meeting from work. And Mother was less than reliable as a source of transportation. Bruce was the "pack chief," an assistant to our pack. Even though he wasn't quite eighteen, they'd bent the rules since he was a seasoned Scout.

Bruce rang the bell in a neat way—two quick buzzes, then one long. Mother answered the door while I gathered my belongings.

Bruce pulled out a bouquet of flowers. "Well, hello, Mrs. Stewart, how are you today? Did you do something new with your hair?" His smile and flattery were about as thick as his glasses. Over the last two years, Bruce had won over my parents by buying them gifts at Christmas, birthdays, and just because.

Basking in his compliments, Mother blushed. "Thank you for the flowers. That was very nice of you."

He sure knew how to charm. It worked every time. Mother lived in a constant state of irritation—especially with Dad. But with Bruce, her face lit up and her mood calmed down. Her cheerful glow resulted in a brief cease-fire in the entryway. I was impressed that Bruce could break through her barrier. If he could make my mother happy, he was special!

With my scarf perfectly adjusted, I grabbed my cap and squeezed past Mother. Bruce put a hand on my shoulder.

"Boy, you look snazzy in your new uniform, Tom," he said. "You'll start earning your skill awards in no time." He turned to Mother. "I'm not sure what time we'll get home, Mrs. Stewart. I'd like to review a few things with Tom afterward, if that's okay with you, ma'am."

She nodded and waved, then shut the door.

I climbed into Bruce's 1970 International Scout truck. The gauges flashed like a pinball machine, and he'd stuck a compass on the dashboard. The afternoon sun cut through the brisk autumn air as Bruce drove down Marine View Drive. I pulled the visor down, not only to block out the sun, but also to see how "snazzy" I looked.

At the stop sign, Bruce turned on the radio and started rocking out to some music that he said sounded "dynamite."

"Yeah, that's dynamite, all right," I said. I wasn't sure what we were listening to, but I wanted to be just like Bruce.

"Are you having a good birthday so far?" Bruce asked over the din of the music.

"Yes, thanks, Bruce." I covered my mouth with my hand. "Oops, sorry, I know I'm supposed to call you 'sir' when in uniform, right?"

"Tom, when it's just the two of us, you can always call me Bruce, but that stays between us, okay?" He pulled a hand off the steering wheel and flew a high five my way. "I have a surprise for you for your birthday."

He swung around to park in front of a burger-and-fry joint called Frisco Freeze. "What flavor of milkshake would you like?"

I chose chocolate; he ordered strawberry. We sat in his truck and gulped them down to the very last slurp. My teeth chattered. "Ugh, brain freeze at Frisco Freeze!"

Bruce snorted and almost spit out what was left in his mouth. Gasping between my own belly laughs, I said, "Thanks for the shake."

Bruce wiped his mouth. "I just want to make my prize Scout happy."

I couldn't believe it. *Did he just say I was his prize Scout?*

Then he laid his hand on my knee. I looked up at him. He was watching me, as if he were in a trance. I glanced away. I wanted to ask him if he was okay, but I didn't.

He exhaled and seemed to snap out of it. "Ready to go?" He gave my knee a little squeeze. It was just like a buddy pat-on-the-back thing, like my dad or grandpa would do—right?

We arrived at the meeting place and parked next to Dad's car. The other new boys were waiting outside the building, unsure of where to go or when to enter. Bruce walked beside me with his hand on my back and led the group inside. *So, this is what being popular feels like.*

Dad was waiting at the podium wearing his old Boy Scout uniform. I'd never seen him in it before, and it still fit him. Dad introduced himself and Bruce and welcomed each boy with a firm handshake. The meeting began with an official roll call, prayer, and formal flag ceremony.

"Normally, we'll discuss any unfinished business and upcoming events, present your skill awards, and do pack activities," Dad said. "But because this is the first meeting, today we'll be going through the handbook."

I was ready. Bruce had been prepping me for the last month. He'd taught me the Cub Scout salute and handshake and showed me how to form my fingers into the Cub Scout sign—the wolf ears. I already knew the motto—*Do Your Best*—by heart and the requirements to earn the first rank of Bobcat. Bruce's instruction had made me feel like an instant adult. No one had ever taken this much interest in me before. Bruce might as well have been Bruce Wayne—a superhero in my eyes. Starved for attention, I sought out approval wherever I could get it. With Bruce stressing what he expected from me, I tried that much harder to be the best Scout possible.

Even though I was only a Cub Scout, I had already memorized the Scout Oath and Scout Law.

> On my honor, I will do my best to do my duty to God and my country and to obey the Scout Law; to help other people at all times; to keep myself physically strong, mentally awake, and morally straight.

The Scout Law said, "A Scout is trustworthy, loyal, helpful, friendly, courteous, kind, obedient, cheerful, thrifty, brave, clean, and reverent."

Bruce had told me, "These traits aren't just for the Scouts. We should live life this way—as moral, ethical, and upstanding citizens."

Dad gestured to Bruce to proceed with the closing flag ceremony, and Bruce nudged me to help him. I stood up a little straighter as I took my place beside him. With my first official Scout meeting under my belt, I politely tapped Dad's shoulder. "Dad, can I ride home with Bruce?"

He nodded, and I headed for the truck, walking about ten feet tall and hoping all the other boys were watching me get in.

The sky-high wishes I'd had for my Scouting birthday were coming true, thanks to Bruce. I gladly absorbed the long-overdue attention he gave me. As we pulled out of the parking lot, I could never have imagined that his destination would take me on a detour to a place where my childhood would no longer be mine.

—∅ Chapter 3
Stained

IT WAS GETTING DARK BY the time Bruce and I left the Scout meeting. The stick-on clock on his dashboard read 8:04 p.m. I reached over to turn on the radio so we could rock out like we did earlier, but Bruce quickly shut it off. His mood seemed different and a little bit strange.

"Did I do something wrong, sir?" I asked.

The last thing I would ever want to do is make Bruce mad. I was used to unpredictable mood swings with Mother, so I knew just what to do—lay low and keep quiet. But Bruce shook his head.

Unexpectedly, he wrenched the steering wheel and swerved off the main drag, sending the two empty milkshake cups sprawling on the floor. I played goalie with my feet, trying to keep the drips left in the cups from spilling all over the mat. Bruce drove along some unpaved side streets where I'd never been before. He slowed to a coasting pace, tapping on the brakes until finally coming to a stop in the middle of the street. He leaned over me to open the glove box, his sweaty armpit in my face. The sweet smell of deodorant mixed with stench made me gag a little. I sunk down in my seat so I didn't smother in his shirt. He was being a little creepy—like when Mother was acting strange—and it was freaking me out.

Bruce pulled out a map and shifted back to his seat, flipping on the overhead dome light to study it. He had told Mother he wanted to review a few things with me after the meeting, so that must be what we were doing. *Should I ask him where we're going? Maybe he's taking me on my first Cub Scout off-road adventure.* Then we started driving up a steep hill.

Finally, Bruce pulled his truck over to the side of the road out in the middle of nowhere. He moved the gearshift to the middle and then from side to side. The truck swayed from front to back until he firmly pulled out the emergency brake to lock it in place. He shut the ignition off, slid the overhead light to the off position, and then turned off the headlights. It was even darker now.

Bruce reached over me to pull the lever that reclined my seat, his elbow brushing my privates. That's what Mother had taught me to call them. She'd also told me never to touch them. I shuddered.

"Tom, I need you to lie down." He guided me backward on the reclined seat. "I'm so proud of my prize Scout. I'm going to give you a massage because you've worked so hard. This is routine for a Scout leader to do with a Scout."

I nodded. I didn't know anything different, just that I would do anything to make him happy. Would this be the first skill award I earned?

Bruce grabbed the bar in front of my seat and pulled it, sliding the seat all the way back so he could climb in front of me. I heard the milkshake cups crumple against the floorboard. Then I felt his hands on my body. It tickled. His gentle touch was something I'd never felt before. My parents were anything but touchy-feely.

Is this what massage therapists do? He sure knows how to give good massages.

"Tom, do you trust me?" Bruce asked.

"Yes," I responded. Even if I didn't, Mother had ground good manners into me. To obey authority had always been at the tippy-top.

"I'm going to adjust your belt buckle. It feels too tight," Bruce said in a soft voice. Click went the brass buckle. "Oops, the button to your pants came undone too." He paused and waited for a response from me.

Should I ask him to stop?

Something didn't feel right, but he was my Scout leader, so it must be okay. I wasn't supposed to tell him what to do. I certainly didn't want to disappoint him.

In a low whisper, Bruce said, "You know how it's a secret that you call me Bruce when we're alone? This is a bigger secret, and it's even more important that it stays between us, okay? You need to remember that."

I saluted him. "Yes, sir, on my honor."

⁂

After Bruce dropped me off at home, I tucked my shirt in and straightened my cap. I didn't want my parents to suspect I'd been "playing doctor" with Bruce. I was afraid if they saw me, my face would give it away. I slipped down the hall to my bedroom. Once inside, I tapped the touch lamp on my desk, illuminating the bundles of old newspapers that had taken over my bedroom, suffocating the space. Mother was a collector—if that's what you could call it. My room, like the rest of the house, was a storage locker. I couldn't figure out why she kept this stuff. I could understand holding on to our first haircut clippings, but *every* haircut? And saving our fingernail trimmings in a jar surely wasn't normal. Mother had more shoes than days in the year to wear them. She packed outdated pairs away in the basement next to the out-of-style outfits that used to complement the shoes. Nothing was ever given away or donated. "They might be back in style someday," Mother always said.

Matt and I didn't have any say about our cells—that is, bedrooms. Nothing was worth causing a reaction from Mother. My small oak desk, squeezed into a corner, was the only spot in the room that reflected part of me. I kept it perfectly arranged, the drawers a haven of order. I suppose I had Mother to thank for its precise tidiness—my reaction to the chaos of clutter everywhere else.

A knock came at the door, and I froze. It was Mother and Dad.

"I'm changing," I said, hoping they wouldn't come in.

"We just wanted to say happy birthday and good night. Love you," said Dad through the door.

"Thank you, and love you too," I responded. *What is this heavy weight on my chest?*

I changed clothes, neatly hanging my uniform and cap on the child-sized clothing rack leftover from my nursery. Turning to the dresser, I rummaged through the top drawer—the only drawer Mother had left for me to use—to find a clean pair of underwear. No luck.

The smell of Bruce's Old Spice was still stuck to me, and that might be just enough to give my secret away. It was probably best to wash the smell off. I quietly opened my door and tiptoed to the bathroom, locking the door behind me. The lock didn't give me a sense of security. Mother had picked the lock and crashed my privacy one too many times. To make sure I'd wiped well enough, she'd say.

I considered taking a shower but decided against it. It would be too much work to move the stacked boxes out of the shower, and I didn't dare get them wet. Mother had tried to convince me that her dry shampoo powder was more convenient, but I knew she just didn't want to dirty another towel, which meant more laundry. I usually settled for rinsing my hair under the faucet. Dad's solution was to go down to the state park once a week and shower in the public bathroom.

Opening the cupboard, I pulled out a bar of hand soap. Next to it sat a yellow bar of Fels-Naptha laundry soap. I shuddered. Fels-Naptha was ideal for treating stains, removing grease, and . . . washing little boys' mouths out. I could still taste the horrible bitter residue on my tongue and the grit between my teeth. "No Stewart will ever use inappropriate language or disrespect me," Mother's voice echoed in my head. I was a pretty good kid. Sometimes I didn't even know what I had said to make her mad. It must have been Matt.

Later, I'd learn that Mother's punishment of choice contained a toxic, cancer-causing chemical. In excess, it was proven to cause leukemia, kidney cancer, and neurological damage. But for now, I was more concerned about how Mother might wield the Fels-Naptha if she found out about what I'd just done with Bruce. Rolling the sweet-smelling bath soap between my hands, I lathered up a washcloth and put it down my pants. But the washcloth didn't get the smell off me. It would take something even stronger than Fels-Naptha to eradicate this stain.

Chapter 4

The Gift of Faith

I MET GOD AT BROWNS Point United Methodist Church. The quaint wooden church was set on ten acres of wooded forest just a few miles from our home. It had been built in the late 1950s, and my parents were founding members. We never missed a Sunday.

This Sunday, like most Sundays, we were late. Mother had scrounged up two clean pairs of corduroy pants for me and Matt and stuffed us into the back seat of our family vehicle, a butterscotch-colored monster of a Suburban named after the 1968 movie *Chitty Chitty Bang Bang*. Behind Mother's back, Matt and I had our own nickname for the gas-guzzling jalopy—one that rhymed and started with the letter *s* instead of *c*. In the front seat, Dad and Mother talked about something called the Jesus movement. I busied myself making plans to lay track for my Lionel train set when we got home. My stomach rumbled, reminding me that I hadn't had breakfast.

By the time we made it into the lobby of the church, I could already hear the strains of music filtering through the heavy oak doors. Thirty minutes fashionably late was on time for my parents. *Here we go again*. Forget slipping into the back row unseen. Mother loved an audience. She pushed through the doors and marched down the center aisle. I followed, mortified as a hundred eyes watched my walk of shame up to the front row. I shrank into the pew and focused on the breathtaking view behind the pastor's pulpit. *If only I could escape into those woods*. Instead, I made my escape to Sunday school class, Matt in tow.

I don't remember the exact moment I accepted Christ into my life, but God gave me the gift of faith from an early age. I had a lot of alone time with God on the late bus home from school, in my bedroom, and in the basement. I prayed often, and God spoke to me through the Bible. The lessons of my Sunday school teachers sank deep into my heart, creating a love for God and a belief in His love for me that would become a refuge amid the questions brewing in my young heart. *Why would You allow Bruce to do this to me? Why does Mother love me for what I do instead of who I am? Do You think I'm good enough?*

The only way I knew to be good enough was to try to make Mother happy. God called us to honor our parents, right? My yes, Mother skipped like a broken record, stuck on a tune I didn't choose. It didn't matter if I was happy; what mattered was trying my hardest to be the perfect son that she wanted. In my best effort to earn her affection, I sacrificed Saturday after Saturday to accompany Mother on her three-hour hair and nails appointments—cut, color, roll, and dry. I sat patiently as if there were no other place I would rather be. I pushed the heavy cart for her at the local supermarket, which was more like a warehouse—one of those stores where you bag your own groceries. I was surprised Mother chose a place like that because she liked to be catered to. But then again, she had me; I wrote down on a piece of cardboard the shelf price of every item Mother put in the basket. I even made breakfast in bed for her on the weekends. I waited and waited for some appreciation in return for my loyalty. Like the Energizer Bunny, I kept going and going, always on standby, always on alert for a simple thank you or, better yet, I'm proud of you. But Mother wasn't one of those nurturing types. She was the one who expected to be nurtured.

Since Mother didn't work, I found it kind of odd how she was rarely ever home after school when we got off the bus. Matt and I spent many afternoons working on our homework in the sheltered patio between the house and garage because she'd left the house locked. Bruce knew I was one of those latchkey kids—just one without a key. He also knew I was lonely. He told me, "You can always count on me for anything. I'll be here for you—whatever you need, Tom."

Perhaps my circumstances pushed me to rely on God earlier than most. I viewed God as all-powerful yet loving. I read the Bible stories about Joseph and Daniel and David, where God allowed suffering for a reason and turned evil into good. I didn't yet know what reason He had for allowing Bruce to touch me or Mother to neglect me, but with the faith of a child, I believed that if He didn't protect me from them, He'd give me the strength to persevere. I trusted that someday I'd see Him bring good from it.

Thank you for my day today, God, I prayed that Sunday morning. *Thank you that I get to stay at school longer for music and sports. Thank you for Virgil and Mrs. Hess and how they make me feel at home. Thank you for my friendship with Bruce. Please, God, help him not be mad at me. I don't know what I would do if he didn't like me anymore. And thank you for Matt. Even though he's annoying sometimes, having a brother makes this all more bearable.*

After the church service let out, I scarfed doughnuts in the foyer, washing them down with as much juice as I could gulp. I wasn't the only one hoarding food. I saw Dad tuck away as many doughnuts as he could fit into his jacket pocket. He was the one who had taught us to sneak whatever food we could fit into our pockets at his favorite all-you-can-eat buffet. At least Mother had enough tact to not swipe anything from the church's silver service—as far as I knew. Dad's job at the American Plywood Association was a good one, but no way could his salary support Mother's stockpiling. She had a habit of snatching up salt and pepper shakers, napkin holders, and silverware from restaurants. At home, towels and washcloths showed up out of nowhere with hotel names imprinted on them. The silver holiday platter in the china hutch had the name Olympic Hotel engraved on it. She came home from shopping trips with armfuls of stuff. Or were they shop*lifting* trips?

I snuck one more doughnut. I wasn't a thief. I was just hungry— hungry for attention, affirmation, and a God whose love was real.

Chapter 5

Target

BRUCE WAS RELENTLESS. I WAS eight and naïve. Bruce was eighteen and depraved. Whenever he could get away with getting me alone, he would do it, week after week, month after month. His truck, our basement, his parents' backyard, the secluded woods near the basketball hoop—he had a portfolio full of creative lies to get me alone, usually related to helping me earn some merit badge. I started to dread waking up in the morning. I waited and waited for someone—anyone—to figure him out. But no one suspected anything. Mother may have been overprotective in a million ways, but she was clueless to this.

When school started the fall before I turned eleven, I was ready to graduate from Cub Scouts to Boy Scouts. Bruce offered to take me to Camp Kilworth to practice for my archery merit badge. I really wanted to learn how to shoot a bow and arrow, but I knew what happened when I was alone with him. Yet Bruce offered me an escape from home—from Mother—that was difficult to refuse. In a toss-up, I'd have to choose Bruce. At least I got to go somewhere, and it was the only way I could fill up my sash. Who else would I be able to learn this fun boy stuff from? Dad was always so busy with work.

Bruce arrived on Friday afternoon to pick up me and my camping gear for the weekend. The camp wasn't far. We arrived at a fenced-off entrance with a big, worn wooden sign overhead with carved-out letters that spelled Camp Kilworth. The gate, which was made from tall shaved-bark tree trunks bound together with rope, looked like an opening to a secret portal.

The truck tires crunched as we drove down a gravel road and stopped in front of the ranger's cabin. A tall woman ranger with a long gray braid came stomping out in big black boots. I didn't know a lady could be a ranger; she looked more like a man.

Bruce looked at me as if to say, Just stay quiet. I was already good at the lay low and keep quiet thing. He rolled down his window as she approached, her expression less than friendly. Bruce turned on the charm. "I'm bringing our newest star Boy Scout here to advance him on some skills. He needs to earn his archery merit badge. I brought my tent, ma'am, and is it okay with you if we find a spot to stay the night?"

"Okay. Just keep your surroundings clean," she reminded us. Her response was enough to make Bruce's face brighten. He looked like he had just earned a merit badge himself. He thanked her twice, and we drove on.

Huge trees lined the twists and turns alongside a river that ran through a deep crevasse. Bruce took his foot off the gas pedal long enough to point out the archery range on the left.

"We won't have time tonight to shoot any arrows. Sorry, Tom. We need to pitch the tent before it gets dark. We'll try our hand at it tomorrow."

He shifted the truck into four-wheel drive and revved up the winding hill, plowing through branches, which clawed at the windows. I clutched the doorframe to keep from hitting my head on the ceiling and laughed.

Finally, Bruce stopped and pointed to a clearing. "This is the perfect site. Let's get to unpacking, my prize Scout."

I pulled my sleeping bag, pillow, and duffel bag out of the truck. Bruce had come prepared with a two-man tent, lantern, and cooler full of food. He was always prepared, just like the Scout motto said. Then I saw him stick a handgun into the back of his pants.

"I had to bring my gun since we are out in the middle of nowhere," he explained.

So why don't I feel safe?

We set up the tent on a cushion of fallen leaves. It didn't take long at all—we had practiced setting it up so many times in his back-yard. I gathered branches for hotdogs and marshmallows while Bruce collected logs for a fire. I had just returned with an armful of twigs when I heard him say, "Oh no, I forgot matches and my lighter."

That's funny. He never forgets anything.

"I'll grab the lantern."

He waved me away. "Nah, we don't need it yet. We can light the fire later the Scout way. First let's get our stuff in the tent."

He handed me our pillows and took the sleeping bags in his arms. We shuffled around to get the sleeping bags and pillows arranged just right. While we were inside, he zipped the tent closed. He patted his hand on his knee for me to come over and sit next to him.

"Since you're my prize Scout, I should be your prize Scout leader, shouldn't I?" he asked.

I didn't know what he meant, but it seemed right to nod my head yes.

"I deserve to feel good too. I mean, it's only fair. Tom, don't you think it's your turn to help me?"

It was a command rather than a question. Bruce looked at me and then down at himself.

Then . . . I knew.

I had never dared to question him or tell him no. I tried to swallow but the spit stuck in my throat. What he was asking me to do was sickening.

I spoke—like an idiot. "Bruce, do I really have to do this?"

Bruce's expression darkened. "Tom, you are to do what you are told. Remember the gun? The one I had in the back of my pants?"

I gulped. Guns scared the bejeebers out of me.

"Do you see where the gun is now? I'm not kidding."

I looked over at where it lay in the corner of the tent.

Bruce's voice had become a growl. "You know, Tom, I don't do all I do for you to get nothing in return. I will never help you or take you anywhere again if you do not reciprocate. I'm sure you wouldn't want me to tell anyone about what I've done with you, right? You wouldn't want your mom or your dad to know. He paused and looked right at me. "Or even Virgil, right? You will do this for me."

"Yes, sir," I said, the word *gun* echoing in my ears.

❦

The birds chirping at sunrise woke me. Last night I'd had a nightmare. In my dream, I'd been naked, and Bruce had pointed his gun at me. I lay still, thinking. Was Bruce what they called gay? Would they call me that too? I knew I wasn't gay—I liked girls. Bruce wasn't hurting me—maybe it wasn't so bad. Most of the time, I enjoyed Bruce's attention. He made me feel good about myself. But those times like last night made me feel so icky and unsafe. How could Bruce make me feel so good and so gross at the same time?

I pulled the sleeping bag tighter to my chin as my breath sent puffs of moisture into the air. My stomach rumbled. We had never started that fire or made dinner last night.

My movement woke Bruce. "You okay?" he asked with a groggy voice.

"Yeah," I said, trying to hide my chattering.

"Good. No wussy Scouts here, you know."

I guessed he meant a coward. Gosh, no way would I want to be that.

"Well, I guess it's time to finally make that fire." He clambered out of the tent, and I heard him fumbling with the door of the truck.

"Guess what?" he hollered. "I found my lighter. How about we make hot dogs for breakfast?"

After breakfast, we packed the truck and cleaned the campsite. I didn't realize we were going to leave so early, but Bruce did keep his promise and introduced me to the archery range before we left. I felt so clumsy. I couldn't seem to hit the target even once. Bruce wouldn't be calling me his prize archer any time soon. As we drove back down the gravel road, Bruce said, "You did okay, Tom."

Okay was never good enough for Mother. But coming from Bruce, it felt like a compliment. I wondered if he meant the archery or something else.

Chapter 6

Growing Up Geek

AT MEEKER JUNIOR HIGH, I engulfed myself in sports. The more time I spent at school, the less time I'd have to be at home. And being an athlete counteracted the sissy harassment I got for playing the viola that Mother made Matt and me play. I was convinced she wanted us to be famous musicians with matching black tuxedos and bow ties. Even though music was Mother's idea, after hanging around the other band geeks for a while, I decided they weren't so different from me. They didn't tease me all the time like the other kids. I was proud to call them my friends and proud to be called a geek right along with them. At first, I'd thought I wouldn't like orchestra, but playing in my first concert was incredible. We geeks sounded great together on stage. Unfortunately, the bookworm and nerd comments kept coming. I was taller than most boys, so that deflected the bullying a bit. But it was my ability to dodge Mother's attitude for so long that helped me avoid bullying like a pro.

Even though I found a home with the band geeks, sports were my passion. I loved basketball. Coaches told me I was a shoo-in and a natural. Since the year before, I had grown to six feet. I could be kind of clumsy in other stuff, but with sports I was focused and determined. A Stewart played to win. Competitive should have been my middle name. I don't know if it was sports that brought that out in me or just my last name. Either way, my pride inflated with each win, especially when the local newspaper published my picture with the captions "star athlete" and "most valuable player." I'd finally found an avenue to access the attention and admiration I desperately craved.

I had all the moves, stealing the ball and taking jump shots. All those street basketball scrambles must have done the trick. But my skills didn't seem to impress Mother. When she showed up to my games, her criticism did too. I never knew if she'd be there or when she'd embarrass me. I could hear her shout from the sidelines, but it wasn't to cheer. "That was an easy shot. I can't believe you missed it! Anyone else could have made that one." Or "You failed your team." It put a damper on even the coaches. I was surprised she wasn't escorted out.

I felt important being one of only three seventh graders chosen for the team. On the day of my first practice with the varsity basketball team, I wasn't feeling well, but there was no way I was going to stay home with Mother. During the middle of a scrimmage, Mother showed up and boldly strode across the court toward our coach, Mr. Walker. He blew his whistle so the players wouldn't run her down. Being tactful and staying on the sidelines was not my mother's way. Mother had everyone's attention—just the way she liked it.

"Hello, Coach Walker. I'm Betty Lou Stewart, the mother of that fantastic player with so much potential, Tom. He wasn't feeling well this morning, so I brought some Tums for his tummy."

My teammates were close enough to overhear what she said. I could have died. Coach Walker crossed his arms, a look of amusement overcoming his irritation. "Well, well, well, player number fifty-three, Tommy Tums." Then he chuckled sarcastically. "Hey, Mrs. Stewart, I could use some Tums for myself. My sissy team is playing so poorly they're giving me nothing but indigestion." Hounded by the laughter, I had a new nickname: Tommy Tums.

The flirty looks from the cheerleaders helped me play better, but I had to focus to keep my eyes on the ball and not their cute little skirts and waving pompoms. I had just turned thirteen, and puberty was in overdrive. Girls, girls, girls! That's all I thought about. My body was changing. I had hair in new places, and there was a new squeak in my voice that sounded so girlie.

Looking in the mirror, I saw a teenage boy as straight as they come—except for my teeth, that is. They were about as crooked as they come. Mother got me braces to perfect my smile—just like she tried to perfect everything else about me. But her haircuts were less than perfect. I gritted my teeth each time she played barber. Butcher was more like it. The always-crooked bowl cuts she gave me left me wide open for teasing. Her choice of glasses for me didn't help matters any. She always chose the biggest, nerdiest glasses that didn't come anywhere close to cool. My concerns were eased when I saw Bruce proudly wearing his glasses. Maybe mine weren't so nerdy after all.

If glasses and braces and a bad haircut weren't enough to label me as a dork, puberty plagued me with a million zits. Mother was determined to solve this. She treated me nightly with every acne cream she could buy off the shelf. None of them worked. That was after she almost squeezed my face off to pop the pimples. Off we went to the dermatologist for the latest and greatest procedures—multiple treatments of lancing with needles, infrared ultraviolet lights, and even liquid nitrogen. It was a grueling process, but I did appreciate Mother's attempts to help me.

With glasses, braces, and acne working against me, just being Mr. Nice Guy was not enough to attract the girls. At least during basketball and baseball season, my status went from dork to jock—and I taught myself on how to use it to my full advantage. A jock with a 4.0 GPA, willing to help chicks out with their homework? A brilliant idea. Wear my Scout uniform to school? Even better. They swarmed all over me, and I soaked up my all-star status. I had to. It was the only thing that allowed me to separate my secret from me. Bruce had confused my already mixed-up understanding of what normal was. My connection to girls was the only surefire way I could reassure myself that Bruce would not ruin me as a man.

Bruce filled me in on everything I needed to know about girls— way more than I should have known. He knew just how to talk in teen-boy language, giving me all the answers to my questions before I even needed to ask. With a smug attitude, he said, "Now, Tom, you'll be prepared for the intimate stuff by the time you start dating girls. You owe me." He showed me girlie magazines with big glossy centerfolds.

The only girl I'd ever seen naked was my mother, who had no sense of modesty at home. Maybe that was her strategy to keep me away from girls. She jackhammered into my brain how I needed to stay a virgin until I got married. *Am I still a virgin?* Mother had caught me touching myself one night. "We Stewarts never participate in any vile acts of crudeness," she had hissed. "Masturbation is a sin, Thomas Gregory Stewart! God's wrath will come upon you if you continue." I'd had no idea what I was doing was bad. I was just a curious teenager with raging hormones. The boys at school always joked about it like it was the cool thing to do.

The subject of sex, and anything associated with it, was taboo to Mother. She pulled me out of sex education at school so I wouldn't be exposed to that sort of dirty teaching. But she didn't know that Bruce had already given me more of a sex education than any class. She didn't know I wasn't her perfect virgin boy anymore. Mother would have damned me to hell if I tarnished the high-and-mighty Stewart name. Programmed by Mother's constant hell-and-damnation warnings at a young age, I had walled off that part of my thought life because it was all considered dirty.

—⁂—

One day as I walked home from school, a groovy black van pulled up beside me. It was Bruce. He rolled down the window.

"Where'd your truck go, Bruce?" I asked.

"Oh, I still have it. I thought I would treat myself to this beauty too. Do you like it?"

There were no windows other than the windshield and driver and passenger side doors. I'd never seen such dark, tinted windows before—like a surveillance van in the movies.

"*Jaws*, the movie, is coming out this Friday at the drive-in. Would you like to go?" Bruce asked. I sometimes wondered why Bruce didn't hang out with friends his own age. He was probably lonely.

"That sounds great," I said.

"Hey, let's bring Matt too."

I wasn't thrilled at the prospect of my younger brother tagging along, but if he were there, Bruce wouldn't try anything. I figured we'd all just have a good old time in the van, stuffing our faces with popcorn and getting freaked out by the movie.

When Bruce picked us up, Matt beat me to the front seat. Reluctantly, I climbed into the back seat, giving up my spot. I tried not to frown. That passenger seat was reserved for me and only me— not my brother. I was Bruce's only copilot. But I wasn't going to let Bruce see me pout.

Bruce parked at the drive-in theater and loaded us up with pizza, popcorn, candy, and a cooler full of grape and cherry soda. I gorged and guzzled—enough to get me feeling sick to my stomach. Matt started talking and laughing and bouncing from all the sugar.

"Matt, you are so annoying. Settle down," I said, peeved.

Really, I just wanted Bruce to myself.

Finally, it was dark enough for the movie previews to start. It would have made more sense for Bruce to park the van so that we could open both side doors to lounge and watch the movie, all cushioned by the blankets he had piled up back there. As it was, we could only see the movie through the windshield. But watching the movie wasn't in Bruce's plan.

Bruce climbed between the front seats to the back of the van and closed the black drape that separated the front from the back. He suggested that I move up to the passenger seat.

"I need to talk with your brother to calm him down a bit. Turn up the volume on the radio so we can hear the frequency for the movie loud and clear."

I wasn't stupid. Jealousy surged through my chest. The very thing I'd feared—I wasn't the only one. It would be years before Matt and I talked about that night.

⏤⫯⦿

Bruce had moved out on his own and began taking me back to his apartment for sleepovers every weekend. On Saturdays, when Mother brought me home from my viola lesson, his black van would be parked in my driveway. He didn't even ask if I wanted to go anymore—he just showed up unannounced. I liked being able to take a shower there. It was kind of fun acting like I was his roommate. But ever since I'd got braces, Bruce had switched up our activities. He became rougher and more brazen. The things he wanted to do now were worse.

On this particular Saturday, I rested my head against the window as Mother pulled into the driveway, not wanting to look up. But I did. And there he was, stepping out of his van to greet my mother.

"Hello, Mrs. Stewart. You look beautiful today, as always." When my eyes met his, he gave me his usual nod. All I could see in that nod was a liar with a sick mind. I couldn't stomach the sight of him anymore, no matter how much he had helped me and done for me.

Mother didn't even ask if I wanted to go. How could I tell her that I didn't want to go over there anymore?

"Mother, I was planning on hanging out with Virgil today."

It didn't work. Her dreaded you-better-not-back-talk-me look answered that one.

"Bruce didn't drive all the way down here for you to be rude, Thomas Gregory Stewart."

Dragging my feet and my viola toward the house, I whispered a prayer. "God, why me? Please help me. Please make Bruce stop."

Why is God not hearing me?

When I returned from the house, Bruce was saying, "I can drop him off tomorrow morning before church, Mrs. Stewart, if that's okay?"

Without a clue, she happily thanked him. "Of course, Bruce. Thank you for taking such good care of my son."

I upchucked a little bit just to swallow it again. Bruce was the one with the gun—and his gun made the rules.

The entire drive, I said nothing. Bruce tried to make small talk. I wanted nothing to do with it. He parked in his driveway and waited for me to look at him. I couldn't. I got out and walked to the front door, head down. Strange vibes blared off him. I couldn't help but look up. It was as if he were drawing me in. His eyes felt like laser beams, pulling me into almost a hypnotic state—which I had come to recognize as my emotions shutting down.

He was not the nice Bruce today. It was like there was some strange dark cloud over him. It felt like evil in that house.

He tailed me to the bedroom and whisked the curtains closed. My body went cold, and I wiped clammy hands on my jeans. Bruce brushed next to me and reached for the doorknob to shut the door behind me. I waited as the seconds went by to see what move he would make next. My feelings were blank. I just felt empty, as if every part of me had bled out.

"Bruce, please, can we stop what we are doing?" I begged.

I should have known that was a huge mistake.

His nostrils flared. He almost spat his anger in my face. He raised a fist like he was going to hit me. Then he reached behind his back and grabbed for his gun, tucked where he always had it in the waistband of his pants. He swung the gun around to give me a close-up view of his threat and gripped my arm. His thumb clicked off the safety.

"You do what I say and what I want, and you will not get hurt. If you disobey or try and run, I will aim, fire, and shoot you. Then, I will shoot your family next."

My desperate pleas for mercy were embedded in his mattress, buried with my stolen voice and the forbidden no. I felt so stupid—him being able to do that to me. But I felt bound by the heavy chains of his threat to hurt me and my family. My duty to keep my family safe was the only thing I didn't feel stupid about. My family might have been a dysfunctional piece of work, but his threats to harm them terrified me. It was up to me, and only me, to protect them in the only way I knew how—by taking it.

I wasn't a Scout anymore. I was a sex slave scared for his life.

The Confession

THE DOORWAY TO THE KITCHEN might as well have been the portal to a dungeon. I stood in the hallway, my heart beating fast as a sense of panic eroded my determination. I could hear her in there. I could hear the gush of the faucet as she filled the teakettle, the scrape of a worn wooden chair as she pulled it in to the table, the rustle of the morning edition of the *News Tribune*. She was probably looking for any articles about her sons' achievements to clip and paste into her "Snips and Snaps" scrapbook, the physical manifestation of the Stewart pride. My life was measured by those pages. I'd been molded into the perfect son, perfect scholar, perfect church kid, perfect athlete, and perfect musician. And, oh yes, the perfect Boy Scout.

That perfection was about to be ruined.

What I was about to tell her would taint her perfect vision of me. Would it irrevocably diminish her impression of me, her prized-possession son? My achievement was the only bond we shared. To share my shame now was to risk losing the only connection I had ever known between us. Should I even risk it? She probably wouldn't believe me anyway. I felt about eight years old again, a shy little boy afraid to get into trouble. This wasn't going to be an acceptable discussion no matter what I said. This talk should have taken place way back then. But it didn't. If it had, would it have prevented what happened to me? Would it have saved my stolen childhood? I had avoided the inevitable for as long as possible, but I could no longer hide behind the perfection I'd tried to achieve for her sake. I'd been crying out for help, but she hadn't heard my silent screams.

I hesitated in the doorway, on the verge of pivoting and tiptoeing back to my room. The kettle's sudden piercing whistle startled me, and Mother looked up.

"What is it, Tom?" she said, walking to the stove and pouring a cup of tea.

My courage caved in. "Umm . . ."

Without looking up, she gruffly cleared her throat. "We Stewarts do not ever use the word *umm.*"

"Yes, Mother. Sorry." I gulped.

Her mood didn't look promising. My determination was quickly reverting to my usual passive response. Our conversations had always been lectures, where my participation was only to listen and agree. But I wasn't a little boy anymore. Straightening up to all six feet three inches of me, I clasped my palms together, fingers tightly intertwined, and finally spoke. "Mother, I have something to tell you. Something really important."

She fiddled with her teacup. I wanted to scream at her to stop. She'd always hammered respect into me, but it only went one way.

"Mother, look at me."

She leveled her gaze at me, taking a sip of steaming tea. I'd grown up with this stare that looked right through me. She squinted, her eyes zooming in on my face, her eyebrows furrowing. With that one look, my body felt like collapsing. I leaned against the doorframe for support.

"Bruce hurt me. He really hurt me. He hurt me for over ten years."

Once the words were out of my mouth, there was no taking them back. I'd done it. I'd finally spoken the secret I'd carried for so long.

Her face registered surprise at first. Then she closed her eyes. *In denial or anger?* I couldn't tell. Without saying a word, Mother walked back to the table and sat in her chair in absolute silence. Mother was rarely silent in a confrontation. It was the rest of us who usually kept our mouths shut. She crossed her arms, and I waited for what would come next. Mom was unpredictable. Her moods were unstable, her responses often full of disproportional rage.

But now, her blank reaction accelerated my frustration. "Mother, do you realize what I'm saying?"

She continued to ignore me, scowling into her teacup. No reaction. No response.

"Mother, did you hear me?" I'd never spoken to her like this before. I strode across the room and slammed my palm on the table. "Bruce molested me. He abused me!"

She exhaled a sharp sigh of disgust. Her back straightened to meet the high back of the spindled wooden chair. A look of repulsion crossed her face. I watched her expression for any hint of where she was headed. Was she trying to process what Bruce did to me, her little boy? *I think she is. Oh, I'm so relieved. She believes me! What was I so afraid of? Why did I wait so long?* Maybe what I endured would be a wake-up call to her. Maybe it would humble her, spark some good in her. Maybe my sacrifice wasn't in vain.

Mother finally looked up at me. Crumpling the newspaper, she slid her chair back, stood, and leaned her face close to mine. "How dare you talk about your Scout leader like that."

The knot of tension in my stomach blocked my breath for a moment. She might as well have kicked me in the gut. *She doesn't believe me.*

I didn't retreat—not yet. The anger rising in my chest was stronger than any I'd felt before, and it emboldened me. "Mother, why do you think Bruce was so interested in helping me all the time? All those Boy Scout badges and patches? I earned them only when he got what he wanted from me."

"You're lying, Tom!" Mother's voice rose in pitch. "Bruce would never do such a thing!"

I tried to keep the desperation out of my voice. "I'm not lying. I wouldn't lie to you. He threatened me with a gun. He said he would kill my family if I didn't do what he said. He said he would kill you, Mother!"

Now we were both trembling. Mother wouldn't back down. I was familiar with how she used her tirades to deflect her guilt. Perhaps she couldn't face the fact that my abuse represented the ultimate failure as a mother: she had failed to protect her son. Denial was probably easier than living with that knowledge. She could deny reality, but I hadn't had that luxury. I'd had to live it.

After a long moment, I looked away. I'd known the risk and taken it anyway. The courage I'd found had convinced me that she would listen. What had happened to me was like a dream I was unable to wake from. I had hoped Mother would invade the dream and wake me, rescue me, and comfort me. I had envisioned her marching straight down to the police station before Bruce even had a chance to fabricate his excuses. She'd be the one person who'd never let anyone get away with endangering her son. Bruce wouldn't be able to compete with the wrath of Betty Lou.

How foolish I'd been.

What kind of mother wouldn't believe their own child? Her denial hurt more than anything Bruce had ever done. I'd had no voice then, and I had no voice now. I retreated into little Tommy, who packed up his soul long ago and concealed his pain. Now, I concealed my devastation at her betrayal. My pain didn't matter—only my performance. I had tried to be the best son possible to her. No disrespect, no disobedience. I never said anything except "Yes, Mother." It wasn't enough. Her denial only compounded the damage my heart had already sustained.

Mother sat back in her chair, and my shoulders slumped. *Maybe she was right. How dare I insult Bruce this way? Should I apologize for even bringing it up?*

I suddenly felt exhausted. I stood and pushed the chair in to the table.

"I'm sorry you feel that way, Mother," I said, void of emotion. I didn't know what else to say. My feet moved robotically to the doorway, then down the hall. On either side hung the portrait gallery of my life—posed photos of me and Matt in our tacky matching outfits, family outings with forced smiles, framed award certificates and sports articles. The shell of my life, more like it. It was all a facade, hiding how dysfunctional we Stewarts really were. I shut my bedroom door on it.

Get over it, Tom. It is what it is. You're not really that surprised, are you?

I was good at shutting out pain and pretending like I was fine. I'd had years of practice. It was the only way I got through each day, plodding toward tomorrow and the hope of an escape—someday. But as I crashed onto my bed, alone with God among the stacks of newspaper, I couldn't block this out. I reached over to my nightstand and pulled out my worn leather Bible. I skimmed through the delicate pages one by one, searching for answers or some message of hope. My eyes fell on Matthew 6:14: "For if you forgive other people when they sin against you, your heavenly Father will also forgive you."

Really, God? I've been betrayed on both ends—betrayed by Bruce and betrayed by the people who should have protected me from him. And Your word to me right now is forgiveness?

Forgiving was the last thing I wanted to do. I wanted my bitterness vindicated, my revenge approved. I wanted God to punish my mother and Bruce.

And then there was "But if you do not forgive others their sins, your Father will not forgive your sins."

I leaned my head back on the pillow and laid the Bible over my chest, my eyes and heart heavy. I'd done my best to be an obedient follower, a perfect son, just like I had for my mother. I felt terrible when I failed God. If I didn't forgive, would I face His wrath too?

I dozed off to sleep. The journey to forgiveness would be a long road to walk.

Chapter 8

Spreading My Wings

BY THE TIME I WAS fifteen, I stopped counting the number of times Bruce violated me. By seventeen and a half, I struggled to keep myself sane. I threw myself deeper into my already stringent schedule of school, sports, the symphony, and Scouts.

I left the summer after my junior year open to concentrate on achieving Eagle Scout. I'd had to take a two-year break after my troop disbanded due to low enrollment. Bruce was running out of excuses for my mom, so he found another troop for me. It just happened to be the same troop he had earned his Eagle Scout rank in—Troop 336. Two years out of the Scouts was such a long time, I worried that earning Eagle Scout was a lost cause. Becoming an Eagle Scout was so important to me—more than playing the viola or any of the sports I participated in. But more than that, to *not* make Eagle Scout meant facing my mother with something she would consider a massive failure. On average, only two percent[1] of Scouts achieved the rank of Eagle Scout, and I was determined to be one of them.

I hadn't come this far just to let it slide out from underneath me. Of course, Bruce was right there by my side to make it happen. Whatever his motives were, I needed his help. I was in the home stretch. In addition to gathering references and submitting a formal application, I needed to plan and direct a service project. Mother met with the firemen at the local fire station and learned that two fire houses needed repainting—an ideal opportunity for an Eagle Scout project for sure. I spent that whole summer painting the Dash Point and Browns Point fire stations, clearing brush, and painting fifty fire hydrants a shiny silver. Dad wasn't involved, but Bruce was more than happy to help out. When I finished, they placed a plaque of recognition on the wall engraved with the words "Courtesy of the Stewarts." I'd done it!

The night of my Eagle Scout court of honor ceremony the following spring, I felt sick to my stomach. As we recited the Scout Oath, the voice coming out of my mouth didn't sound like mine. *"On my honor, I will do my best to do my duty to God and my country and to obey the Scout Law; to help other people at all times; to keep myself physically strong, mentally awake, and morally straight."*

Morally straight? I had a problem when I got to that part. Wasn't morally straight the opposite of immorally gay? I knew for sure I wasn't gay. Because of that, I hated the stuff Bruce made me do. Bruce was keeping me from being morally straight and forcing me to lie like he did. Would I eventually become gay because of how much he had done to me? Could I still recite the oath if I were not fully telling the truth? Would I have to hold my hand behind my back with my fingers crossed? I had always obeyed authority—but to do so, I couldn't tell the truth. Which rule did I disobey?

Is that okay, God? Does my sin count if I was being threatened with a gun? Maybe God would excuse that one.

In Scouts, God was at the forefront. I was doing my duty to Him—obeying authority and following all the other rules—so why was God not protecting me from what Bruce was doing to me? Because of the heavy burden of achievement in my life, I approached God with the same transactional nature of my human relationships. If you are good, He will love you. If you are perfect, He will protect you. Was God not answering my prayers because of my shame? Though my faith remained intact, my questions to Him had become increasingly desperate, even angry. I prayed, asked, begged, and pleaded for God to take this horrible man away from me. I was growing weary and weaker each time Bruce took advantage of me. Why was God not answering me?

Bruce called me up to the stage.

"Let's give it up for the man of the hour, Tom Stewart—my prize Scout!" The other Scouts in the room looked on and clapped with envy.

Bruce draped me with compliments in front of everyone, showing me off like a trophy. That's what I was. Bruce gestured to me to model my sash full of merit badges, pointing out each one and explaining how I earned them. I'd earned them all right. I'd earned this swimming badge in the pool locker room. I'd earned this archery badge in his tent. I'd earned this camping badge in his backyard. The longer I stood next to him at the microphone, the more my journey to get here came back to me. The story in my head sounded quite different from what he was telling everyone else.

When Bruce handed me the official Eagle Scout certificate, I turned toward Mother with a robotic smile so she could snap a picture. Bruce took my hand in a firm grip, an outward acknowledgment for achieving Eagle Scout. But my handshake back was more of an inward congratulations to myself that against all odds—despite Bruce rather than because of him—I had endured. *Thank you, Lord.*

After I earned my Eagle Scout ranking, I began to see Bruce less. Now that Scouts was off my schedule, he must have lost interest in me. I wondered if little boys were more his flavor. I could never figure out why a man would choose to be with a boy in the first place. All this had to eventually come to halt sometime, didn't it?

⟿

My senior year was a whirlwind. I plowed into college applications, traveling to prestigious universities of Mother's choosing and taking multiple entrance exams and SAT tests. Mother revved her engines and did whatever it took to maintain my superior Stewart status in the high school's select top ten seniors. She was relentless with her need to see me acquire scholarships, awards, recognitions, medals, and honors. All that constant preparation fast-forwarded me to my upcoming graduation. I was so exhausted that I didn't even go to prom. No time and no date for me anyway. Whatever college I decided to attend, I knew the distance between Mother and me would replenish some of my missing peace of mind. But, more importantly, Bruce couldn't follow me there.

One afternoon that spring, I headed down the stairs to the basement of our house, the wooden treads squeaking under my feet. Only a sliver of light came in through windows set high on the wall, so I flipped on the light switch, shivering as my bare feet met the concrete floor. Dad's workshop area had been overrun with Mother's junk. Along the wall sat an old, gray sagging sofa opposite a broken sink and the fireplace we never lit. Across the room through the double glass doors was a small bedroom with a single bed next to an old side table with a lamp on it. That was where Dad slept when Mother was mad at him.

Piles of applications covered one side of the ping-pong table in the center of room, each neatly addressed, stamped, and ready to mail. On the opposite side of the torn net sat stacks and stacks of the assignments and tests I'd held on to, accumulated since seventh grade. I'd lined them up adjacent to each other, collated by grade and then by class. Nothing less than all A's, just as Mother demanded.

I sat down at my ping-pong workstation and looked across at the couch. This basement was both a dungeon and a refuge. Bruce had taken advantage of the privacy of this room to perpetuate his abuse. He was the only person Mother had ever let inside our penitentiary of a home. But this same seclusion had become my sanctuary for studying, reading, journaling, and praying, offering solace from the family dysfunction upstairs. I felt close to God in this room. Here I could feel genuinely loved as His son—and pretend I wasn't hers.

Looking over the stacks of what would fuel my future, I saw my mother in a new light. My academic success was a byproduct of her relentless pushing. Her drive, misguided as it may have been, had fueled me all along. Learning to tune out her voice had given me a special ability to concentrate, focus, and bury myself in my schoolwork, no matter what was going on around me. She encouraged me and, by exasperating me, steered me to find my own purpose. Her expectations had kept me out of more trouble than I realized. I'd never disobeyed, never smoked, never drank, never got into any trouble.

Though I still resented her in so many ways, a bud of thankfulness sprouted in my heart.

On graduation day, Mother emptied an entire roll of film on me dressed in my graduation cap and gown. The braided honor tassels and the gold medallion around my neck told me again: against all odds, you did it.

The strains of "Pomp and Circumstance" filtered through the air of the auditorium as the procession began, and I made my way to sit on the stage as one of the top ten students in my class. The hundreds of other graduates, outfitted in either yellow or blue caps and gowns, took their places on the floor. I squinted into the bright lights. The room was filled to the rafters, but no one could miss my parents tirelessly waving their programs in the air. Were they really proud of me? Or was it just the old Stewart pride making sure everyone noticed that they were the ones who had the son with the word *covaledictorian* printed beside his name?

This was what I'd worked for. This was the payoff. I glanced back out at my parents. This was what I was supposed to do—make my parents proud. Right? I heard my name called, felt a firm handshake, heard whistling and cheering. And suddenly I had a diploma in hand. My smile for the camera was genuine this time, and my watery eyes told me that my emotions weren't completely dormant. I looked down. It was as if I had to see it on paper to believe it. It wasn't the list of achievements that filled me with awe, it was the fact that I'd endured and overcome.

Thank you, Lord, for getting me here. I think I'm going to be okay.

It was unbelievably freeing to toss my cap into the air along with the rest of the graduating class of 1981. Something had eased in me during this rite of passage. My bitterness toward Mother was slowly deflating. She'd pounded in demands for perfection, but I had been honored because of it.

Chapter 9

Rising Up

I WOKE UP EARLY THE day after graduation, not knowing what to do with myself. I couldn't remember the last time I'd slept in. I looked over at the diploma propped on my desk, and then it dawned on me: Bruce hadn't been there last night. The last several months Mother had kept me so busy that Bruce had stopped coming by. Did that mean the threat to my family was over? I'd learned to wall off all thoughts of him when we weren't together. But now, familiar feelings of shame sprang up.

Tom, you were just plain old naïve and dumb. I thought back to the time Matt and I went with Bruce to the drive-in. *Matt was so much smarter than you—smart enough to keep his distance from Bruce before he sank his claws into him for keeps.*

I was startled by the doorbell. *That's strange. No one ever comes to the house.* No one except for one person. The two short buzzes and one long raised the hair on my neck. My parents had gone out. *No, Lord—please! Please, make him go away.* I could just sit here, not move a muscle, and pretend that no one was home. But Bruce probably knew I was here. He always made sure to know where I was. Most likely, he'd watched my parents leave without me, waiting for the opportune time to come and pay an unwelcome visit.

The bell rang again.

I needed to face him, the same way I'd faced Mother. I shot up a quick prayer as I walked to the door. *Lord, be with me.* I peeked through the peephole, and there he stood, looking like his usual frumpy self. Trying to appear calm, I opened the door, keeping the opening narrow by planting my size-thirteen foot as a doorstop behind the door. I winced as I looked at the man standing in front of me. I wanted to lash out at him and say the worst words I could think of, but keeping it cordial was a better idea.

"Hey," I said, even though many far worse words came to mind.

He nodded once and eased forward to invite himself in. My foot stayed put, keeping the door where it was.

I attempted to detour him. "I was just heading over to Virgil's house."

Bruce paused with a predictable sigh. Annoyed, he waited for me to open the door, looking at me with a blank expression but saying nothing. We stared each other down. I wasn't giving Bruce his customary welcome or the on-cue compliance that he had become so used to. He was like an incessant bully, but he'd taken so much more from me than lunch money.

He had the gall to push his body against the door, inserting his foot across the threshold as leverage.

I stood firm. Pulling together all the courage I never knew I had before, I boldly said, "Bruce . . . No!"

Bruce scowled as he attempted to barge through. I'd never experienced how he would respond when he didn't get what he wanted. Confronting my mother earlier had uncovered some buried bravery in me. Even though she hadn't believed me, finally standing up for myself had unlocked something in my soul.

"Bruce!" I yelled. "No more. I am done! You will not get near me again. You need to go away for good and leave me alone."

We glared at each other without flinching. Suddenly, panic rose in my chest as his gun came to mind. I'd forgotten about it. *Does he have it in the back of his pants?*

No sooner had the thought appeared than I felt the pressure of his foot against my foot lessen. He stepped back without a sound, turning his back on me. *Thank you, Lord, he doesn't have the gun.* He didn't seem angry—just disappointed, in a pitiful, pouty kind of way, like I had just broken up with him. I watched him leave, his posture slouched and his feet dragging down the driveway.

My body trembled. All I wanted to do was yell after him, "Why did you do this to me?"

I quickly shut and locked the door, a torrent of emotions taking over. An unfamiliar feeling of pride swept through me—not the Stewart kind of pride, but a much-needed self-esteem boost from standing up for myself. But I also felt like crying. *Why in the world would I feel sad?* Then delayed regret hit me the same way it did that morning when I confronted Mother. I relived the same remorse: How dare I insult Bruce like that? How could two people who had used me and hurt me both make me feel as if I were the bad guy? I tried to make sense of it, but my thoughts were all jumbled. *What's wrong with me?* Why did it bother me so much about Bruce walking away the way he did? Why did I feel like I betrayed him? Why did I feel so guilty about making Bruce feel bad? He had used and abused me for more than half my life.

I mulled over my conflicted feelings. Then I remembered an incident we had talked about in one of my classes after a local teenage girl had been kidnapped. She had been pulled into a van while walking home, repeatedly raped, and then held captive for a week before being released. Her reaction to the incident was not what people expected. *What did the teacher say she showed signs of? Didn't it start with an S?* Grabbing my encyclopedia, I thumbed through *sickness . . . symptoms . . . syndrome*—*that's it.* I read down the listings until I came to *Stockholm syndrome*:

> A psychological response wherein a captive begins to identify closely with his or her captors, as well as with their agenda and demands. . . . Psychologists who have studied the syndrome believe that the bond is initially created when a captor threatens a captive's life, deliberates, and then chooses not to kill the captive. The captive's relief at the removal of the death threat is transposed into feelings of gratitude toward the captor for giving him or her life. . . .

It takes only a few days for this bond to cement, proving that, early on, the victim's desire to survive trumps the urge to hate the person who created the situation. The survival instinct is at the heart of the Stockholm syndrome.[2]

When I'd first heard the story of the kidnapped girl, I had been fascinated. I now understood why. Survival. I'd developed the same traumatic bond with Bruce to survive the last ten years of my life. I was starting to put the pieces of my own life together.

Chapter 10

Leaving the Nest

DAD WAS HEAD OF PERSONNEL at the American Plywood Association, and he used his connections in the industry to get me a summer job as a factory worker at Reichhold Chemical Company in Tacoma. My duties involved playing backstop for fifty-pound bags of wood preservative flakes called pentachlorophenol as they slid down a chute and off a conveyor belt to be sealed for shipment. I had to be on high alert. If my attention drifted, I'd get sucker punched in the gut. Sealing and stacking the bags on pallets was a strenuous, nonstop job. Good thing I had some stamina and endurance from sports.

My other responsibilities included vacuuming out the heavy powder that lined the furnace and cleaning out the formaldehyde liquid pits. There were stringent safety precautions due to the hazardous conditions. Employees were required to wear safety glasses, protective coveralls, arm guards, and gloves at all times. Still, the airborne odors and flying penta dust made me feel loopy so I couldn't focus. It was especially hot that summer, and with all that gear, I might as well have been wearing a sauna. Since I was tall, sometimes the protective clothing didn't cover all of me, exposing my extremities to the toxic chemicals. The toxins absorbed into my skin like a sponge, but I didn't think anything of it. I just wiped it off and continued earning my pay.

It was the hardest job I'd ever done, but I kept plugging along. Dad had helped me get it, so whining or complaining wasn't allowed. Besides, I didn't want it to give Dad a bad name for referring me. Dad's job was his life. It defined him and stroked his ego. When introducing himself, he would take a deep breath, puff out his chest, and make sure the other person knew he was the top dog in the wood products industry.

At the end of each workday, I was drenched with sweat and dehydrated. I slept in the basement where it was cooler, but the sweat continued to pour out, no matter where I slept or how cool it was. I'd wake up several times a night to soaking wet sheets, awake but in a state of delirium—not conscious of where I was and with the same loopy feeling I had at work. If I did fall back asleep, I would drift straight into a nightmare about Bruce. I'd wake again, begging God to help me get back to sleep. With my recurring night terrors, I dripped more sweat down in that basement than I ever did on the production line.

When September hit, the loopy feeling remained. I gave my notice since I'd be off to college shortly. I'd received scholarships to attend the University of Washington. Mother was thrilled that I had chosen a local college close enough for her to visit. Still, moving to a dorm on campus would allow me the much-needed space I never had. I'd had my wings clipped for so long I was ready to spread them and soar.

The day I was to leave for college, I woke to the smell of breakfast. Mother had unexpectedly fixed my favorite meal of scrambled eggs with cheese. I was just surprised Mother had cooked at all. I threw my legs over the side of the bed and sat up. *This is it. I'm really getting out of here!*

I was packing my suitcase when Dad rapped on my door. Another surprise. *What's he doing home? Did he stay home from work today?* I wasn't used to him being home. Like clockwork, his daily grind began before the sun came up for his all-consuming career.

"Come in," I said, folding a shirt into my suitcase.

As he entered my room, his eyes probed mine. "Do you have a minute?"

"Sure. Everything okay?" I moved over on the bed to make room for him to sit down.

Sit-down conversations between us didn't happen that often. When we did talk, it was usually to casually catch up or simply shoot the breeze, so this caught me off guard. It wasn't like him at all.

"I remember when I was your age, Tom, graduating and heading off to college," he started. He chuckled and murmured something about wanting to give me some "valuable fatherly advice" before I left the nest. It was the same chuckle that often preceded his launching into a familiar story. There was something different in his manner this time, and I leaned forward.

Dad grinned in his easygoing way and rested his hand briefly on my shoulder. He started in on how great things were way back when—but they must have been before I was born because my way back when had never been happy.

"Remember what happened the night before my graduation?" He shot me a quick glance to see if I was with him. "When everything went wrong for me? When my dream of walking with my graduating class wearing my burgundy cap and gown with the gold honor tassels ruptured just as my appendix did?"

I could have told Dad's story verbatim from memory, but I liked hearing him tell it, so I humored him.

"Tell me again," I said, with memories of my own graduation just three months ago fresh in my mind. Maybe this time Dad would reveal parts of the story he had kept to himself. There had to be something more to this Stewart saga I'd been born into.

"So . . . with the only ambulance in town called to another emergency, the medics needed to find an alternative mode of transportation to the hospital. They called the most unlikely but feasible option they could think of—the local funeral home."

He laughed at the memory. "Yes, a hearse. I thought they were joking. They weren't. There I was on a stretcher. Stay flat, they told me. I couldn't do much else besides freak out. The medic tried a little morbid humor. 'Well, young man, if your appendix ruptures and we can't get you to the hospital in time, your body will be all ready for the coroner. I'm kidding of course.' That's when I passed out."

"That sounds painful," I said, folding a pair of pants and laying them neatly in the suitcase.

"Excruciating," Dad replied. "But I forgot all about the pain when I opened my eyes to a stunning nurse with bright-red lipstick leaning over me. Betty Lou."

I couldn't help giving a small laugh. It was difficult to picture my mother—the collector—in a clean, sterile environment like a hospital.

Dad had a faraway look in his eyes. "Yes, your mother was a year older than me, but we flirted up a storm. She had a calming peace about her. The way she moved around my bed helped me drift back to sleep. I fell into a dream of my mother coming to me and leaning over my bed in the same way. Your mother was the first lady who had comforted my soul in a place that had been empty since Grandma had to leave."

I nodded. I knew his mother had been committed to the Western State Mental Hospital when he was thirteen. I wondered when the advice part was coming.

Dad paused, and I noticed the new lines in his face, etched with the weariness of the world. Marriage to my mother hadn't been easy. He ran a hand through his hair, now salted with gray.

"I've heard somewhere that men sometimes seek out women who are like their own mothers. Please listen carefully, son . . . Be very, very cautious with your choices." He looked me straight in the eye with a meaningful look. "You know what I am saying, right?"

This part of his rerun of the love story was different than usual. He must be warning me to never marry someone like Mother.

I nodded. "Yeah, I do."

"Good. Well, we've got to get going soon. You finished packing?"

I pulled the zipper around the suitcase. "Yep."

Dad hefted it up while I grabbed my duffel bag. Taking one last look at the bedroom of my youth, I pulled the doorknob, shutting the door on a past I couldn't change.

Matt met me at the front door, giving me an awkward hug. "I'll miss you," he said.

"Yeah, me too," I said, clapping him on the shoulder. I felt a prick of guilt. I was getting out while Matt remained trapped. My brother and I had grown close, despite our competitiveness and the fact that Mother favored me over him. He was a loyal friend, and we shared the bond of brothers who had faced the same adversities.

With the trunk of the Dodge Aspen all loaded up, I folded my frame into the backseat. I'd run out of time to say goodbye to Virgil. Maybe I'd avoided it. I'd miss my friend terribly.

I could see Dad's face in the rearview mirror, looking in deep thought from the driver's seat. I looked over to see what kind of look Mother had on her face, but she wasn't in my view. When we got down to the bottom of the road and passed Bruce's old house, I deliberately looked away. I sure didn't want a whiff of that man clinging to me.

No one said much during the hour-long car ride. After we arrived at the campus, my parents helped me unload. As we walked down the corridor to my dorm room at the end of the hall, Mother started in on her usual "Remember to . . ." and "Don't forget to . . ."

"Yes, Mother," I said to each point she stressed.

Inside the room, Dad quickly put down the suitcase, appearing too antsy to stay. He made his usual man-to-man goodbye to me and gave a quick "Love you." I had never seen him cry, and today was no exception.

"I'll wait for you in the car," he said to Mother on his way out the door.

Mother stepped in front of me, grabbing my hands and looking into my eyes. Instinctually, I put up my emotional barriers.

Surprisingly, tears started streaming down her face. As she sobbed, my resentment traveled toward understanding. My mother had hurt me in ways that might never be repaired. She couldn't undo the past. I couldn't say I'd forgiven her yet, but something had changed in my heart. At this moment, the many years of what I had perceived as criticism from her crystallized into the message "I'm proud of you, son," like a rough stone smoothed into glass by the sea.

That made my own tears flow. I pulled her into an embrace, and we wept together. This was the first time I had ever felt that she actually loved me. I hugged her tightly like a little boy needing his mommy. When I released my bear hug, it released eighteen years of suffocating spite. I grabbed her hands again and said, "Thank you, Mother. Thank you."

Chapter 11

Discos and Diamonds

COLLEGE WAS A LITTLE OVERWHELMING at first, but I was prepared for that. Mother had conditioned me to tackle obstacles. I wasn't sure how well I'd fit into the college social scene since my reclusive manner held me back from stepping out. I'd heard that living the famed frat life was a sure bet to hook up with a girl. Here was my chance, or so I thought. Fitting the mold of the fraternity type was just not in my makeup. I still hadn't drunk a drop of alcohol, and smoking was definitely out of the question because I knew how many carcinogens were in cigarettes. No amount of peer pressure would get this boy to party. No matter how much I wanted to fit in, I wouldn't falter. I suppose I had Mother to thank for that. I was a good boy to the bone.

Nevertheless, with my need for approval skyrocketing, I continually sought out the admiration of others and attempted to fit in. The hereditary Stewart pride was becoming a dominant trait in me the older I got. I used inappropriate humor as a crutch to seek attention. Oh, I got the attention all right, but it backfired. My insulting sarcasm ran off any girl who may have wanted to spend time with me. It didn't take me long to realize I needed to tone down my weirdness and my cocky side to even come close to mingling with the opposite sex.

My lust issues were growing too. Surrounded by half-naked college girls prancing around didn't make it any easier. Frat life seemed to be measured by as much association with women as possible. I'd daydream about a harem of hotties flocking around me to fulfill my every desire, but I knew that would only happen to me behind my eyelids. I think my yearning for the girls to swarm around me was pathetically obvious. Countless girls accepted my awkward invitations for a date but then rapidly made their getaways after the first date, which didn't help my already fragile self-esteem.

A battle began between my physical desires and my spiritual convictions. My commitment to and active involvement with Campus Crusade for Christ helped me through the murky waters of temptation. I sought the attention of women because, behind it all, I feared that Bruce had changed me completely as a man and I might never change back. I had to prove to myself that Bruce hadn't stolen my charisma. Maybe I never had any in the first place. My braces, zits, and glasses were a thing of the past, so that wasn't it. What was it about me? It was as if the girls sensed what had happened to me and did whatever they could to steer clear of me. The aroma that Bruce had left behind—the one I'd tried to wash off that first night in the bathroom—still hung over me.

I was incredibly lonely. Being single on a Friday night with nothing else to do, I attended the weekly dorm dances. I'd never gone to school dances in high school and hardly listened to music. I'd only just begun to discover the music of my generation—Journey, Foreigner, and Elton John. Since I rarely had a date, I usually went stag with the other honor students—the same type of band geeks and nerds I'd clicked with since grade school. It just felt comfortable being one of the nerdiest among the nerdiest. We huddled together and competed to be the first to get a girl to dance. We either got a pass or fail. If one in the bunch got lucky enough to slow dance with a girl, he passed with honors. My competitive spirit rose up the same way it had in sports. I was determined to be an all-star ladies' man.

On this particular night, I'd rehearsed my best pickup lines and put on my Stewart swagger. Only five minutes into the dance, I met the gaze of a girl across the dimly lit room. She moved confidently toward me, sweeping curly, shoulder-length brown hair behind her ear and flashing me an adorable smile. She stopped in front of me and introduced herself.

"My name is Amy. Yours is Tom, right?"

I was surprised she knew my name. I looked down at her and suddenly felt less like a nerd. I just felt really tall.

"Yeah," I said eloquently.

Before I could formulate more words, she said, "You wanna dance?"

Over her shoulder, I saw one of my buddies raise his eyebrows and nod. *A-plus!*

She grabbed my hand and pulled me to the middle of the dance floor. We stopped under the twirling disco ball, surrounded by flashes of bright strobe lights. They illuminated her brown eyes and reflected off her glasses. I wished the deejay had played a slow dance instead of a fast tempo so I wouldn't be embarrassed by my clumsiness, but my body actually grooved to the beat. When the song came to an end, we huffed and puffed to catch our breath.

The instrumental start of the next song made my pulse beat harder. The party lights dimmed to match the mood of the ballad. If there were ever a song meant to help a guy land the girl, it was "Open Arms" by Journey. A hint of romance sparkled in Amy's eyes, and in one smooth motion, she set us in motion by draping her arms around my neck and nestling in. Chills rushed up and down my body. I didn't know this could feel so good. Before, arousal had always meant something else, something dirty. Not anymore! I was more than relieved with our immediate connection on the dance floor. Our slow dance together felt so natural, the way it should be between a guy and a girl. Maybe I didn't need to worry about my confused testosterone.

Amy loosened her hold around my neck. She looked at me, then leaned in and pulled my head down for a kiss. I'd never had a girl go in for the kiss first before. Amy's forwardness was refreshing. The applause I received from my audience of guy pals up against the wall added to my confidence.

Our mutual, easy laughter shattered the rest of the ice that needed to be broken.

Our relationship progressed quickly. Amy was in a sorority just down the street, and she was smart like me. That became the basis of our relationship, what we had in common, and I used it as my cover.

I was buying time for the inevitable, stalling for the next stage that Amy boldly hinted at. I couldn't bear the thought of her fleeing like the others, but the thought of not waiting until marriage to have sex bothered me just the same. She admitted she wasn't a virgin. I didn't care either way. The dilemma I was struggling with was whether or not I still was.

My convictions were keeping me strong for the time being, but I felt my willpower weakening. I knew as a Christian I shouldn't even go there, but not knowing if I was even able to perform as a man haunted me even more. When the time did come to be intimate, would I be too damaged? I really loved Amy. I wanted to marry her. But marriage meant sex and sex meant Bruce. I was having trouble separating the two. Somehow, some way, I had to sever the memories of Bruce from my future, but how to do that without actually having intercourse, I didn't know. *Don't mess this one up, Tom. Don't scare her away. Don't say anything stupid.*

Amy didn't know what she was in for. Amy wasn't like my mother, but any girl who was with me would have to compensate for my mother-wound, a hurt that made me desperate for love and nurturing.

Inevitably, I had to introduce Amy to Mother. Amy was Norwegian like us, and I knew Mother would like that. I gave Amy the rundown before we made a weekend visit home. One thing hadn't changed—Mother still didn't have visitors in the house because of her hoarding, which was fine by me. I didn't want Amy to see the embarrassing stash of stuff anyway. Instead, my parents had parked a small Shasta trailer in the orchard next to the house for us to stay in.

Mother looked Amy up and down, evaluating her. She must have passed muster, because Mother invited us into the trailer, where she'd laid out her fine china to impress Amy. Arranged on the plates was Mother's idea of an elegant meal—Norwegian goat cheese on crackers with a side of liverwurst. I waited impatiently for Mother to make her exit so I could begin executing my plan.

"Well, I'll leave you to it," she said at last, slamming the trailer door behind her. I pulled out a chair for Amy, and she slid into it gracefully. I took my place across the wobbly table, then reached over and took her hands. We didn't even think about touching the food laid out before us. I had rehearsed my lines many times but paused to prevent any desperation from entering my voice. Stroking her fingers with my thumbs, I sat up straight and began.

"Amy, I love you." Her eyes stopped me when they welled up. Her tears were more touching and poignant than any answer to a proposal I could have imagined. I gently eased my right hand away from hers and reached down to retrieve the ring I had hidden under the seat cushion next to me. As I rummaged for it, it slipped off the seat and bounced with a faint clang onto the vinyl floor. That move was not in my master plan.

With feigned nonchalance, I got on the ground to retrieve the diamond ring, then pivoted onto one knee. *Yeah, I meant to do this all along.*

Amy stretched out her left hand, weeping. "Yes!" She grabbed ahold of my shaky hand to help slide the ring onto her finger, then guided me by the elbow to stand up with her. We hugged each other tightly and tenderly. My heart soared. I never thought any girl would want to be with me, let alone marry me. Taking charge, Amy stepped across the floor to flip down the lever on the door into the locked position. I froze. *Moment of truth. Where's Mother? She's probably watching from the house with binoculars. Thank goodness the curtains are drawn.*

"Are you prepared?" Amy asked.

I'd considered that this might happen, so I'd made a stop at the drugstore down the street, purchasing my sin-before-marriage precautions and dashing out the back door before anyone I knew might see me.

What I wanted to tell her was, I'm an Eagle Scout. Our Scout motto is Be Prepared. *Of course I'm prepared, Amy.*

But adding my dry humor to the moment was probably not the wisest of remarks. So, I stuck with "Yes, I'm prepared."

Really, I was terrified. This wasn't how it was supposed to be. But Amy needed to know how broken I was in this area before we took our vows and married. If it turned out my manhood was too messed up for her after we were married, that truly wouldn't be fair. I reasoned my way out of my guilt. Amy wanted it, and I'd always done what the woman in my life told me to do. I let my urges take over.

The entire experience was corrupt long before we even started. But damn it if I would let Bruce steal this too. He may have stolen my childhood, but heck if I let him steal my manhood!

―✤―

Unfortunately, Amy's yes was short-lived. I don't know if she got cold feet or if it was the stress of both of our mothers that did it. Maybe it was my deepening faith, which was going in a different direction than her own. Whatever it was, there was nothing I could say to change her mind.

In the daze of being dumped, I walked my humbled pride over to a pizza parlor near campus with a sudden craving for an olive, hamburger, and pineapple pizza. I slumped into the corner booth and pulled out the glittering token of my love that Amy had returned, studying it. *Why is it me again who is the single guy sitting all alone? Prize Scout, prize athlete, prize academic . . . now I'm just a prize fool. What's wrong with me? Why am I such a loser?*

As always, I shut off my feelings. I nestled the ring back into my button-down shirt pocket as the server delivered my quick-fix pizza therapy. Placing a napkin on my lap, I bowed my head as I usually did. But the words that entered my mind weren't my own.

Tom, I halted the hamster wheel you've been on to make you stop and be still.

Startled, I glanced up and around to see who might have been talking to me. The room was empty.

At any other time, the end to my prayers over my food gave me the ready-set-go-ahead to dig in. Not this time. I pressed my cupped hands back to my forehead, waiting to hear something else.

You survived Bruce's abuse. You survived your mother's pressure. You survived Amy's breakup. Your suffering is not in vain. I can use it for good.

Then there was quiet. I felt cradled in amazement as I embraced the message. *I know it's you, Lord. I hear you loud and clear.*

I walked out of the restaurant with a take-out box full of untouched, lukewarm pizza and more peace than I had ever felt before. Little did I know how much I'd need that peace in the coming months.

Chapter 12

A Dark Haze

NEAR THE END OF THE fall quarter of my sophomore year, I was wrestling with my friend Kent in my dorm room when our roughhousing got out of hand and I hit my chest on the edge of the bedpost. It knocked the wind out of me.

"Are you okay?" Kent asked when I didn't get up.

I didn't want to cry in front of Kent, but I couldn't help it, the pain was so intense. I managed to drag myself into bed and curl into a fetal position.

"You don't look so good," Kent said, concerned. "You should go get checked out at the campus health clinic."

"You're right," I said. Maybe I had fractured a rib or something.

I went to the clinic the next morning. An x-ray didn't show any fractures, but it did show something else that concerned the doctor—a dark haze hovering near my heart and lungs. He told me I should see my primary physician right away. I'd be home soon on Christmas break, so Mother made an appointment for me.

Both she and Dad accompanied me to the appointment. Dad, absent for so much of my childhood, was able to come because he'd recently lost his job. First, the doctor called for an MRI. The grim look on his face told us the results. Then he scheduled me for a biopsy. A pit formed in my stomach. I knew what that word might mean. A shadow hung over our Christmas celebration as we waited for the results. When they came in, they confirmed my fears.

"It's Hodgkin's lymphoma," the doctor said.

Cancer? I took deep breaths to calm the swell of hyperventilation rising in my chest. Mother's frantic bellowing drowned out what the doctor was trying to say. I held my head in my hands, feeling the full weight of the diagnosis. I could do nothing else but pray. *How do I get through this, Lord?* It was difficult to hear myself praying over the sounds of Mother's crying. The doctor handed her a fresh tissue to replace her tear-soaked one.

The doctor started to explain my options for treatment, but I wasn't listening—until his voice lightened up. "You're lucky, Thomas, as we caught it early—stage one. The probability of remission is very high." He added, "If you had been diagnosed any later, it most likely would have been fatal."

I looked upward. *Thank you, Lord.*

In the car on the way home, I felt an undeniable peace. I had felt fragments of God's presence before, but never had it registered as powerfully as it did driving down that road.

I stayed home through Christmas break and used the time as a sabbatical to make sense of what was ahead of me. I revved up my prayers. *Okay, Lord, I'm now still enough to hear you. I am milled down to nothing. I'm waiting for what you want me to do through this.*

Mother didn't take it as well. After I returned to school, she continued to be severely depressed by my diagnosis. She leaned on me for support, calling me often to express her ragged emotions. She'd sigh helplessly and whimper, "I can't even get myself out of bed, Tom. The stress is too much for me to bear."

I didn't have the heart to remind her that it was me who was starting radiation treatments, and it was me who had cancer. I patiently listened on my end of the receiver—as long as it took to pacify her worries. That's one thing she'd taught me as her son, an infinite amount of patience. It reminded me of those many Saturdays I'd spent as her companion. I tried to reassure her I was in the best place possible for treatment, living right there on campus. But her phone calls were becoming a burden. In the back of my mind, I couldn't help but wonder, *How could you dismiss Bruce's abuse but be devastated over my cancer? Why do you care now?* Still, I was determined to resist acting disrespectful toward her. A confrontation like that would have been a bigger battle than fighting off my cancer.

One night in early January, I slid my journal out from the nightstand, opened it, and pressed the seam flat to write. Journaling was a habit I'd held on to ever since those days in the basement. In black pen, I spelled out the word CANCER in all capital letters at the top of a fresh page. No matter how you said it, that word was scary. *Okay, Lord, please take it from here.*

I scribbled down everything that came to me, verbatim.

You were meant to be assigned that dorm room.

You were meant to wrestle with Kent that night.

You were meant to hurt your rib.

I stopped writing as it sank in. . . . *Oh my goodness, I get it.* These circumstances had been no accident. God had taken an unfortunate accident and turned it for good. This could be my own personal miracle in the making. I could see the Lord's hand all over it.

I continued to write all the way down to the bottom of the page until it ran over to the next page. I wrapped up my revelation with this note: "I'm leaning on you, Lord. I'm letting my faith rise above my fear."

If anyone's childhood could have prepared someone for something as trying as cancer, it was mine. I was determined to take one step at a time and do whatever it took to beat this disease. First up was a CT scan, which located exactly where the cancer was attacking me. Next came radiation. The technicians dotted a map onto my chest so they would know where to aim the radiation. It was definitely not the kind of tattoo I imagined I would get. Radiation treatments lasted for over three months. I wasn't sure what was worse—the constant nausea and puking or the painful tests and treatments. I cringed when the technicians inserted dull, three-inch needles into my chest and implanted tubes into the tops of my feet. To distract myself from the agony of this procedure, I fostered an intense curiosity about the process. I was fascinated by how the doctors sent dye into my lymph node system and the images that appeared as a result. I'd loved chemistry in high school, and at the urging of my chemistry teacher, John Gosnell, I'd decided to major in chemical engineering. You don't get more up close and personal with chemicals than with cancer treatments.

Feeling so tired and sick most days, I had to emotionally and physically force myself to get up and go out. I knew I could easily fall into a martyr complex, so I reminded myself that others were going through this too. I'd made friends with the other cancer patients whom I saw on a regular basis. They could relate in ways no one else could. Our shared battle forged bonds that exposed emotions I'd walled off for a long time. Growing up, my parents' emotions had felt artificial—now even more so in light of the raw, life-or-death feelings I was experiencing.

I dreaded going to treatment, but not just because of the radiation. What was even worse was arriving to find out that that another patient I knew had died since I last saw them. I'd never lost anyone before, never experienced grief like this. Along with the families who lost their loved ones and the doctors who lost their patients, I experienced a powerful dose of sorrow, confusion, and anger when I lost my new friends. Yet God always reminded me to refocus back toward Him and use my circumstances as an opportunity to spread His word.

I did just that. I shared with the other patients verses that were comforting me. Psalm 147:3 was one of my favorites: "He heals the brokenhearted and binds up their wounds." In the midst of it all, I sensed God's purpose for me. If God had rescued me from Bruce, I knew God could do it again with cancer.

Remarkably, through it all I maintained a high grade point average. I don't know how—other than with God's help. On alternating nights, I would study intensely, leaving maybe five hours to squeeze in some sleep. The next day, staying alert and awake in class was almost impossible. Then the next night, I'd need at least ten full hours of sleep to rejuvenate enough to function. Missing class was not an option. Quitting school did cross my mind every once in a while, before common sense kicked in. Quitting school meant I'd have to move back home, and that wasn't an alternative I wanted to consider.

With my treatments scheduled in the mornings, I could make my classes in the afternoon. But I'd often feel nauseated in the middle of class, running out to vomit in the chemistry lab. I learned quickly that the bullying I had endured much of my life hadn't yet ended. Jokes about me began to filter through campus. When my hair started falling out, it clumped in the shower drain. The guys laughed and pointed at me, joking that it was my pubic hair left behind. Even cancer couldn't stop their cruelty.

Come on people, grow up.

I managed to keep myself together until junior year. I'd been accepted into the chemical engineering program, but I was having difficulty focusing. The content wasn't more challenging than any of the other prerequisites I had completed, but for some reason, I couldn't think clearly. It was as if my brain were on lockdown. December rolled around, and final exams arrived. My confidence went in ahead of me and reality followed. I blew the test—just blanked! Sitting in my chair, I stared at the test on my desk with no idea how to answer the questions. Going from an A to a C on an exam wasn't going to go over well with Mother. *What's wrong with me?* Something had to be wrong. Worse, when Mother found out, she would *make* something wrong with me. My greatest fear had always been doing poorly in anything.

My first real failure—because that's what a C was in my book— was just as horrible as I had imagined. Mother was hellish. She accused me of conforming to the sinful frat lifestyle and blamed me for downright carelessness. In her eyes, this was pure disrespect, a personal insult against her every expectation for me to succeed. "My next move, Thomas Gregory Stewart, will be to rip you out and away from that peer pressure if you don't improve," she threatened. I had to find out the reason for my failure, if only just to get some relief from her. Fueled by her threats, I headed straight to the doctor's office, where I relayed all the strange symptoms. More tests ensued.

"Your thyroid is dangerously low, Tom," the doctor said. "I'm glad you came in when you did. This could have been fatal."

This was the second time I'd been told I could have died. *Really, God? Why me?* If He'd kept me around this long, He must have plans for me.

Further tests concluded the radiation treatments had scattered to my thyroid and killed it off, but my vital organs had all been protected. Once prescribed medication, my ability to function gradually returned. Faced with the undeniable truth about my thyroid, Mother owned up to the fact that her accusations had no relationship to my grade and instantly zipped her mouth. She had nothing more to say on the subject. My trials seemed to be breaking down the pride of my parents, a glimmer of humility growing in the sacred walls of the Stewart pride.

Even without the pressure from Mother, getting that C on my final didn't sit well with me at all. But it wasn't the grade I was worried about. My cancer treatments had derailed my degree track, causing me to fall behind in my class sequence. That spring, I paid a visit to the office of my mentor, the chair of the Chemical Engineering Department. Professor Sleicher, a balding man in his sixties, sat behind a large mahogany desk. I sat in an uncomfortable chair across from him.

"Please, sir," I said, leaning forward in earnest. "I don't want you to pity me, but I've faced some extraordinary obstacles this year. Please, can you show some consideration for my circumstances?" I was prepared to beg.

He placed a pencil back into a cup on his desk and eyed me. "Maybe you should take a leave of absence and go home until the next quarter starts."

I gulped so loudly he must have heard it. "Sir, with all due respect, may I please ask what my other options are?" My voice cracked. I think he could see the desperation in my eyes and felt sorry for me. At least I hoped he did.

His expression softened. "Not keen to go home to your mother?" he said in an understanding tone. He spoke carefully, but I felt his compassion. He continued. "Tom, I've received an overabundance of phone calls from your mother inquiring about your performance—so many that I've memorized her phone number and now don't answer her calls."

I exhaled. Leaning back in my chair, I raised my hands in a help-less shrug. We both couldn't help but laugh. The professor pushed his glasses up his nose.

"Tom, this is what we're going to do. Since your classes aren't available until next quarter, you may audit some classes so that you can stay on campus. No credits will be granted, there will be no tests given to you, and no homework will be due, therefore, no studying. A freebie of sorts."

I could have kissed his shoes, my anxiety about going home vanishing completely. It was no slam dunk, but I was still in the game.

Chapter 13

Cleansing

DAD PHONED ME LATE ON a Sunday night. Still half asleep, I scrambled for the phone. Dad seemed hyped up, talking fast about an article he'd run across in the newspaper. His angst accelerated with each word. I could hear Mother muttering some not-so-kind words in the background.

"Listen to this, Tom," he said in a shaky voice. "People working in factory-type settings are being exposed to cancer-causing toxins without their knowledge."

Of course, he was referring to the chemical plant I had worked at before college. His voice got gruffer.

"It says here that some employers were aware of these conditions but chose to be haphazard about the safety of their workforce. These companies neglected to caution their employees about the potential dangers of carcinogen exposure."

Understandably, Dad was mad. Mother was even more furious. I was wide awake by now, as I connected the dots. *Was that where my cancer had come from?*

Before I could respond, Dad shouted, "If it weren't so late, I'd be speeding over to my attorney's office."

Mother squawked, "No one will ever put a Stewart in harm's way and get away with it. That damned chemical plant. And damn you, Bob—you got him the job there."

Dad couldn't muster up any rebuttal.

Their squabbling left me feeling squeamish, just as it always did. While the brunt of what Dad had just dropped on me settled in,

I waited for him to collect himself, hoping Mother would shut up for once and stop interrupting. Thankfully, her hollering tapered down.

Dad sighed. "We're going to make this right and go after the plant."

I twisted the phone cord around my finger. This didn't feel right. "It's in God's hands, Dad, not ours. Vengeance is His."

I knew the reason Dad wanted to pursue legal action. His motivation, the same as Mother's, was usually for personal gain. It was the Stewart way. All I wanted was to be free of this family inheritance that had staked its claim upon me. Nevertheless, there was nothing I could do to stop Dad's push or Mother's pull. Those two stubborn Stewarts would insert themselves to get what they wanted with no regard to anyone in their path. But even if their motivations were misplaced, maybe blowing the whistle on the lax safety hazards of this company might prevent someone else from contracting Hodgkin's the way I had. In the end, I knew God would do what He wanted with this, His way. I was completely relying on that to heal me. Going to court and suing the chemical plant wouldn't heal me.

Out of curiosity, I asked Dad to read the toxins listed in the article. He rambled down the list, which included the expected pentachlorophenol, until he came to the last one. It was naphtha—the same ingredient in that toxic soap Mother had used to wash out my mouth. I didn't think that Mother's soap scrubbing days had caused my cancer, but it probably didn't help.

I flinched and hung up before her guilt turned to blame. I didn't want to drift into finding fault. After my firsthand exposure to so much death in the cancer wing, where coping with heartbreak was the norm, everything else seemed petty in comparison. As it was, two other close friends of mine had also been diagnosed with Hodgkin's. None of them worked at the same plant as I did, but I was curious as to what they might have been exposed to along the way. One had passed away, and the other wasn't taking it seriously and refused to listen to me.

I knew I needed to immerse myself in my studies while continuing to pray for that miracle. Best to let Mother and Dad do what they were going to do and stay out of their way. I knew Dad needed a purpose after losing his job. And, well, Mother needed to prove she was right. I just hoped they'd exhaust themselves before doing anything rash or expecting me to join them on their trek for revenge.

Dad's plan of action never came to fruition. I had some blood work done, and the sample analysis came back with nothing definitive. There was no pentachlorophenol detected. If there had been, it would have been proof enough for legal action. If there had been traces, they'd been diminished by the radiation. For me, this was a relief. I didn't want to be a part of their scheme in the first place. But my parents actually seemed disappointed. Perhaps it was the disappearing dollar signs.

It was only a few months later that I sat with them again in the small exam room, dreading what news the doctor might bring. A soft knock came at the door, and the doctor entered, holding my chart. He brushed by and took his spot on the rolling stool in front of me. I swung my legs like an impatient child anxious for show-and-tell. With a slight grin, he opened the front cover of my file. "Well, it looks like the Man Upstairs has more important tasks for you in this world, Tom."

All my words stuck in my throat just like when I had first found out the bad news. The doctor continued. "No chemotherapy necessary." My normal first reaction was to look to Mother for what I was supposed to feel, my emotions programmed to respond to hers. This time, I immediately looked straight up. Goose bumps prickled my arms, and in a rare show of emotion, tears spilled over. I didn't normally cry, but my time in the cancer ward had changed me. And the goodness of God in that moment simply overwhelmed me. The doctor clapped me on the shoulder and added one more wonder to my miracle. "Being able to have children someday should not be an issue. Your reproductive organs were spared."

Kids? I hadn't thought much about that yet. I was just happy to have a future at all. More than relieved, I stood up. The doctor and I exchanged wide smiles. I hugged him as tight as I could. I wouldn't need to see him again.

~ᴿ⊕

That Sunday, tingles of exhilaration ran through my body as I sang praises to God in the front row of my college church, piping out the words of "Amazing Grace" in my own out-of-tune melody. Thankfully, I was drowned out by the piano, but God heard me. I knew He didn't care what I sounded like. Worship felt different today, like I'd been living in black and white and the world had now turned to color. Words I'd sung by rote for years struck me afresh. My gratitude for a new lease on life brought everything into focus. Things had been hard for so long, but now, the future appeared bright.

The church body prayed over me that day. As I knelt down, they surrounded me and thanked the Lord for His favor on me, their hands resting on my shoulders. As they prayed, I murmured my own silent prayer. *You carried me through Bruce, Lord. You comforted me in heartbreak, and You cleansed me of cancer. Thank You for bringing me through the darkness.*

Chapter 14

Taking Flight

I ADJUSTED MY TIE AS I walked toward the monstrous gray concrete building fronted by floor-to-ceiling windows. Leaving the summer sun outside, I pushed through the glass doors into the spacious lobby of the Boeing plant in Renton, Washington. A receptionist glanced up at me from behind a gleaming counter.

"Can I help you?" she said.

"Uh, yes, I'm here for a job interview," I said, smoothing my jacket.

She consulted a clipboard. "Tom Stewart?"

I nodded.

She gestured toward an older Asian woman standing near the elevator. "Ms. Gilmer is ready for you."

"Thanks," I responded.

I had high hopes for this interview. Freshly graduated with my bachelor's degree in chemical engineering, I'd been interviewing for as many positions as possible. The industry was down this year, and jobs were in short supply. Boeing was a big name in Washington. I'd already passed an initial interview just to be here today. If I could land this job, I'd have my foot in the door.

Dorothy Gilmer greeted me with a smile. "You must be Mr. Stewart."

I stuck out my hand, and she caught it in a firm grip before punching the button for the elevator. "I'll take you on a quick tour through the factory on our way upstairs."

I followed her into the elevator and then out onto a walkway overlooking the massive factory floor. Bodies of Boeing 757 aircraft hovered over a polished floor while workers scurried around like ants.

"Do you know anything about airplanes?" Ms. Gilmer asked.

"No," I said sheepishly, "but I know about chemical engineering."

She smiled. "Of course. Right this way."

We exited through a side door and crossed through a sea of lime-green desks. The open office space looked like it had been decorated in the 1950s. Ms. Gilmer led me to a private office, and we settled on either side of a desk. She pulled out my resume and glanced over it.

"So, tell me, why do you want this job, Mr. Stewart?"

"Well," I started, "Boeing sounds like a great company to work for. I've always had an interest in chemistry. But especially so after my bout with cancer."

Ms. Gilmer looked up. "Oh?"

I told her my story. Whatever I said then and in the rest of the interview must have been enough to impress her, because I got the job. A few short weeks later, one of those lime-green desks became my own.

The primary responsibility of my new job was to test chemicals to find safer alternatives to the carcinogens currently used in Boeing's processes. During production, the aluminum airplane parts had to be chemically treated in liquid immersion tanks in order for paint to adhere to the surface. The primary chemical in this process was chromium, a known carcinogen. A typical day for me involved setting up experiments on the computer and then running them in the chem lab or shop. This job was no coincidence. God had put my personal passion into action. As a cancer survivor, I hoped that my work would prevent others from experiencing what I had. I kept a verse on my desk at Boeing—Genesis 50:20, from the story of Joseph. "You intended to harm me, but God intended it for good to accomplish what is now being done, the saving of many lives." My trust that God would use my experiences for His good was finally coming to fruition.

Sharing an open office space with my new coworkers was quite an adjustment since I'd done most of my studying alone. It was a far cry from those solitary hours in the basement growing up. I typically needed quiet to concentrate, and here you could hear everyone's conversations. But I got along with my supervisors and enjoyed my coworkers. My main workplace was in Renton, but I frequently traveled to other Boeing sites for projects. I worked closely with Steve Mason, who led the Hazardous Waste Minimization group. The cast of characters in his group was something else. Sonny Vanderford, one of his technicians, would pretty much sit at his desk half the day and watch other people. He often complained about another technician named Val Brustad who would fall asleep in meetings and at his desk. "Look at this, Tom," Sonny said one day, pointing to a grease mark on the wall behind Val's desk. "He needs to get an oil change more often!"

I played computer golf at lunch with Dave Curran, another engineer, and had fierce ping-pong matches in the chem lab with Harmit Lamba. I'd show up wearing a Michael Jordan jersey to intimidate him. He was a good player with a terrific smash, but I could return them, which made him mad—so mad that he took off his turban and put on a beanie! He said his religion allowed him to take off his turban during athletic matches.

When I wasn't playing around with my coworkers, I spent a lot of my time at Boeing's Auburn shop in particular. This was where the plane wing skins—aluminum wing parts up to one hundred feet long—were chemically treated prior to painting. First, the wing skins were immersed in a thirteen-foot-deep stainless-steel tank full of hazardous chemicals. The second step in the process was known as the deoxidizer step, whereby a little bit of the aluminum oxide layer was chemically removed in a chromium solution. I spent a lot of time testing an iron deoxidizing alternative called Aldox V, and in the early 1990s, the Auburn wing lines replaced the chromium deoxidizers with Aldox V—the first ever significant chemical change in the Auburn wing line.

Another project I worked on was at the Boeing paint hangars in Everett, Washington. The entire airplane rolled out of the Everett factory and over to the paint hangars covered with a green temporary protective coating on the fuselage. Once in the hangar, it was chemically treated to prepare it for painting. In a sense, it was a spray version of the Auburn tank-line process. However, since the 1960s, the deoxidizer step in this process had required mechanical abrading with red Scotch Brite pads that would take eight painters about eight hours to accomplish on a 747. As a result, many of the painters had carpal tunnel surgery. The goal of my project was to come up with a safe chemical that the painters could spray on the fuselage and rinse off with water, instead of scrubbing it by hand. The name of the product was Chemidize 727ND, and it was eventually implemented in all the Everett paint hangars, improving the ergonomic impact on the employees. Like my project in Auburn, this was the first significant change in the Everett surface preparation process.

I threw myself into my work and was eventually promoted to lead engineer. My job kept me occupied, a welcome distraction from the lingering ghosts of the past. It was good to keep my mind busy, and my compartmentalized way of thinking helped me focus on what was in front of me. I considered it a gift that I could block out the trauma I'd experienced. As I got established in my career, a new distraction entered my life—in the form of a woman.

Chapter 15

Bombshell

I DUCKED OUT OF THE rain and into my car, sliding behind the steering wheel and clicking on the wipers. They began a smooth glide across the windshield. Shifting the gear into drive, I pulled out of the driveway and drove down the dark street, heading for the highway. I wasn't yet sure where I was headed. After I'd graduated from college and started at Boeing, I'd moved back in with my parents until I could afford a place of my own. Now that I'd spread my wings and experienced a little freedom, living back at the house was even more suffocating. Tonight, like many nights, I'd made my escape before Mother drove me crazy, searching for a place to walk off the stress and find some peace.

On a rainy night like this, the only dry place I could think of was the mall. I didn't much care for the mall, but it was better than an evening with Mother. The drive over gave me time to clear my head, and I arrived at the bright lights of the mall before more shadows could creep into my thoughts. It was a weekday evening, so the mall wasn't crowded. I pushed through the heavy glass doors and started down the main aisle, glad to stretch my legs. I window shopped, but nothing looked interesting—that is, until I saw a beautiful brunette working in the department store.

I'd promised myself after Amy that I wouldn't put myself in a position to fall again. It hurt too much to be dumped. But loneliness had set in and prompted me to make a move. I didn't want to pass this up. I walked over to the Men's Department where she was working. I didn't need any jeans. But if I were going to meet her, I did. I shuffled my feet to catch her attention. That didn't work. Then I made my way around to the other side of the display where she was organizing. I spotted her name tag—Ruth.

Making sure I was in plain sight, I rummaged through the neatly stacked piles, pretending not to be able to find my size . . . even though I passed over three pairs that would fit me just fine. Finally, she noticed me.

"Do you need any help, sir?"

I opened my mouth, only to discover that the pickup line I had planned to use had picked up and walked away from my memory.

"Uh, I can't seem to find my size."

"Oh, what size are you?" she said.

I told her. With a sideways smile, Ruth reached over and immediately found my size.

I peered at her name tag, as if I hadn't already. "Well, there it is. Right under my nose. Thank you very much, Ruth. May I call you Ruth?" *Oh shoot, I sound formal, like my dad.*

"Sure. I can ring these up for you if you're done shopping."

I followed her to the cash register and made small talk about my prestigious position at Boeing, hoping it would impress her. If her smile was any indication, it worked. I was mesmerized by the way she handled herself. At the register, I stalled to be able to spend more time with her, hoping my compliments would snag her phone number. It worked! Before she handed me the sales receipt, she wrote her digits on the back. I winked to say thanks and headed for the door, a pair of jeans I didn't need under my arm and my washed-out ego rejuvenated. I strolled out to my car, noticing that the rain had stopped. She must be a God thing.

Ruth and I had a whirlwind romance, and not much time passed before I wanted Ruth to take my last name. I retrieved the rejected ring from my first proposal and readied it to take the risk. I didn't want to look desperate, but I also didn't want her to come up with an excuse to run like my first fiancée did. So, it was time to spice up the Stewart charm that got her attention in the first place and pop the question.

I was the happiest man on earth when she said yes. We married just a few months later on Valentine's Day.

While I enjoyed newlywed life, my parents' marriage was on the rocks. Had been for years, probably, but things were coming to a head. Mother and Dad had been married for more than thirty-five years. In all the pictures from their wedding, they looked so happy, but perhaps those smiles were as forced as mine in the family portrait hall.

Dad came over to visit one evening, settling onto the couch in the small apartment where Ruth and I had set up house. My parents had just celebrated their wedding anniversary, so he reminisced about their wedding at first. Typically, after the wedding part of the story, he'd sigh, look away, and his voice would trail off. But he kept going this time, clearly burdened by something.

"Unfortunately, Tom, soon after your mom and I got married, she resigned from her promising nursing career. Even as the man of the house, I had no say in the decision."

Well, that's not much different from today.

Dad seemed more open than ever before. The look of confusion and deep-seated pain on his face was the same as the one he wore when he'd told me of his own mother's mental illness. Dad's mother had been institutionalized when he was thirteen—the same age Mother had lost her own mom. I'd always wondered why my parents acted the way they did. Now, I saw two hurting people who'd lost their mothers at an important age. It explained a lot.

"You know," Dad said, his voice low and laced with sadness, "those once-happy days were short-lived and soon became pure frustration for me. After we were married, not only did she quit her job, she hired a housekeeper and bribed a neighbor to come in the house and bake for her. What was supposed to be a happily ever after became me living in a world according to Betty Lou."

I knew there had to be far more, or maybe far less, to their relationship than he ever let on. Being their son, I could see a disconnect in their souls as they drifted apart. It sounded to me like Dad was more of a father to Mother than her husband. A cold feeling went through me as I thought about what he had gone through for so many years. I admired Dad for sticking by Mother. No matter how many times she hurt him, he never talked about her with disrespect.

"How did you do it, Dad? How did you keep going?"

Dad smiled. "Well, having children helped. You were a long-awaited and welcome change."

Trying to lighten the mood, Dad shifted forward to their making-babies story. I squirmed. It was awkward to think of my parents being intimate. He reminded me of the difficult time they had conceiving. In fact, they'd struggled with infertility for over nine years.

"Finally, as you know, on October 6, 1962, nine years, six months, and two days after Betty Lou Hansen became Mrs. Robert Cecil Stewart, you arrived, Tom." Dad stopped talking and looked down at his hands before he continued. "Something drastically changed in your mother then. It was troubling. Being a new mother must have weighed heavily on her."

We sat in silence. I didn't want Dad to stop talking—he had never been this open before about anything.

"So," I asked, "did things ever get any better?"

He shrugged his shoulders and shook his head. "By the time that she finally had you, she was already thirty-four and then thirty-six when she had your brother. I don't know if things got worse or just more peculiar."

I wanted to commend him on his loyalty and tolerance as a husband in their marriage, but Dad wasn't done yet. "With Matt also being an October baby, she wanted to name him Huckley! So, we'd have a Tom and Huck." He snorted. "That was one time in our marriage I put my foot down! I believe that was the only thing she ever conceded to me."

I was sure Matt appreciated that. "You never told me that part of the story before."

For the first time, I separated my history with Mother long enough to consider Dad's solitary position as her husband. That explained why he was so attached to his work. I, too, had done anything I could to avoid being at home—like deliberately taking the hour-long bus ride home from school. I looked at Dad with new eyes, feeling sorry for what he had gone through. We'd both been weighed down for so long by her overbearing attitude, exhausted from never living up to her expectations. Once I took the focus off my own painful past, I could understand why Dad had been so absent from the family. I had resented his passivity and absence. Now, I felt ashamed for judging him.

Dad stood up, looking lighter than when he walked in, as if he had come to terms with feelings he had padlocked at his core for too long. Maybe he had accepted not receiving in return the respect he gave his wife. He extended his hand to shake mine—his equivalent of a hug. "I am proud of you, son. You've done an excellent job."

"Thanks, Dad." Dad's approval meant everything to me. I walked with him to the door. He paused in the doorway, hesitating before turning back toward me and dropping the bombshell.

"Tom, I'm divorcing your mother."

Chapter 16

The Purge

MOTHER DID NOT TAKE THE divorce well. Throughout the long, grueling divorce proceedings, her health deteriorated quickly. I was her crutch, and she used me to the limit as her support system and later as her taxi driver when she was no longer able to drive. Her demands took a toll on my marriage. Ruth wasn't keen on the amount of time I spent caring for my mother because it infringed on our time together. I felt torn between the two most important women in my life. They both needed me.

It appeared Dad had been planning his midlife crisis for quite some time. I understood him. Having been smashed down nonstop for that long, I was sure he wanted to see how it felt to feel good about himself for once before he got too old. I could relate. But I did appreciate him sticking it out as long as he did until Matt and I were grown. Matt had moved out now too, and he had plans for his future that didn't include Mother. Matt and I had been able to leave; Dad hadn't—until now.

In the years after the divorce, Mother gave up her will to live, a slow suicide of sorts. One morning, when I pulled up to her house— my childhood home in Dash Point—an ambulance sat at the curb. I threw the car into park, jumped out, and jogged across the yard to the front door. It was ajar.

"Mother? Is everything okay?" I called, taking a peek in the kitchen and a swift glance down the hallway. A paramedic appeared.

"Are you her son? She's going to be okay. She's in the bedroom."

Mother lay propped up on pillows in the bed, looking as sick as I'd ever seen her. By the looks of her thin frame, she hadn't eaten in days.

Her face brightened when she saw me. "Oh, Tom, I forgot you were coming. Do me a favor—hand me that bottle on the dresser."

I stepped across the room and picked up the white bottle of painkillers. It was almost empty. "Mother, how long have you been taking these?" I said, concerned. "I thought your prescription ended."

"Oh, I don't know. I've been in pain for a long time. I need my pills."

"You know these are addicting, right? You shouldn't be taking this many."

She popped a couple pills in her mouth and swished them down with water from the glass on her nightstand. "Oh, let off me, Tom. It's just a couple pills."

I wasn't about to let this slide. "Mother, this is serious. This—." One of the paramedics tapped me on the shoulder, and I stepped into the hallway with him.

"We're going to need to take your mother to Tacoma General Hospital," he said.

I nodded. "Okay."

Mother and I never finished our conversation. That was the last time I saw her. After a stint in the hospital, she was transferred to Park Rose Care Center. She'd only been there a few days when Matt abruptly took her down to California to live with him. I tried to call and talk to her but to no avail. She died of pneumonia several weeks later at the age of sixty-eight. Deep down, I believed she died of a broken heart.

The day that Matt called to tell me Mother had died, I didn't know how to feel. *Do I cry? Do I sigh a sigh of relief? That sounds horrible.* Her death was probably not the best time to revisit old feelings. I loved her, I did, but her death felt something like release. I had come to forgive my mother, but I had a lifetime of memories embedded in my emotions. I wasn't sure I wanted to dig them up.

I shut out the grief I was supposed to be going through, just like everything else. Besides, there was a bigger job at hand: drudging and sorting through thirty years of Mother's hoard, which still cluttered the family home. I arrived before Dad and Matt the weekend we'd set aside to tackle the debris. Cracking the front door open, I stepped inside and peered around my childhood home. It felt different with her gone. For the first time, the dread of Mother's badgering wasn't there. So much anger had spewed out of her mouth, it must have soaked into the walls. In the silence, I could still hear the echoes. Tension engulfed me. The feeling was as tangible as it was when I lived there, and I actually called out, "Is anyone here?" But the house was empty.

Alone, I took a last tour around the house, reminiscing room by room. The photos on the wall reminded me of a few good times—mostly from my graduation and Eagle Scout celebration. I deliberately saved the basement for last, the eerie place where so much abuse had taken place. I hesitated before turning the doorknob, praying that God would rid me of what prevented me from seeing beyond my own pain. Especially now, with Mother gone, I wanted to be more thankful for what the good, the bad, and the ugly taught me—rather than what the bad and the ugly did to me.

With each step that I plunked down, I felt a dense cold roll through me. I knew right away that the unnerving chill could not be coming from anything good. I'd felt these same chills when Bruce did his thing. "Lord, I beg you. Please make his presence leave this place. Please take these memories from me."

My prayer was interrupted when the hinges on the front door upstairs squeaked as it opened. Must be Dad and Matt. It was time to rid this basement of the bad and the ugly. Boldly, I commanded any evil there to flee. "Satan, get out of my way and get out of this house." Leaving the rest up to God, I sprinted back up the stairs.

Dad, Matt, and I spent a full two days clearing out Mother's stockpile. We all tried not to show our disgust, but we couldn't resist a few wisecracks. Any formerly empty spaces were now chock full. To sort through everything was a massive chore, but I was glad we had the opportunity. Having a hoarder for a mother also meant that she kept every important thing about my life that I had shut off. I boxed my belongings to take home. She gave me the chance to look back at my childhood through what lay in those boxes, without Bruce blocking my view. I felt grateful to her for that. When it was all said and done, it took two commercial-sized garbage dumpsters crammed full of more than four-hundred jumbo-sized, heavy-duty black garbage bags to dispose of the evidence of Mother's thirty-year hoarding addiction.

With Mother in heaven, I had an opportunity to let go of the past. She was a stronghold who kept me bound to hurts in my history. For so long, my psyche had been plagued by the lie that if I didn't excel or get an A-plus in whatever I did, I wasn't good enough. My trials had taught me otherwise. Without Mother's lens, I could look at my trials not as failures but as opportunities to grow. I thought of James 1:2–4, which says, "Consider it pure joy, my brothers and sisters, whenever you face trials of many kinds, because you know that the testing of your faith produces perseverance. Let perseverance finish its work so that you may be mature and complete, not lacking anything."

I'd persevered through a lot already. But I couldn't say I'd experienced the pure joy James wrote about. I hoped there would be some of that ahead.

Chapter 17

Bundles of Joy

IT WAS A FREEZING DECEMBER day when Ruth called me at work.

"You should probably come home. I think it's time to go to the hospital."

My heart leaped. "You're sure? I'm leaving now."

In one movement, I swept my things together and headed for the parking lot, poking my head into my boss's office on the way out to let him know I was leaving. Ruth and I had been thrilled to learn that our efforts to conceive had been successful. The doctor had been correct when he said my cancer radiation hadn't affected my fertility. After a long nine months, I was ready to meet my son.

The next several hours were a blur of anticipation until finally, in the late afternoon hours, Brian Christian Stewart made his entrance into this world. When Ruth handed me the little bundle, the world seemed to melt away. I walked over to the window of the hospital room, where I could see the snow falling softly outside. So, this was what joy felt like. In his little face I could see myself starting over—a second chance. Despite all the evil and suffering I'd experienced, he was innocent, and I had a chance to protect him the way I should have been.

I stroked his cheek. "Hi, little guy." Would he be tall like me? A lifetime flashed before my eyes—I could already picture him as a basketball all-star, see him earning his Eagle Scout, and watch him graduating from college.

Having a son changed my life, and Brian soon had siblings, Benny and Becca. My daughter was the first Stewart girl born in over a hundred years! My three miracles showed me the first glimpse I ever had of unconditional love. They loved me no matter what. I was their daddy. The most important gift I could give my three children was to tell them about the life-changing power of Jesus Christ. All three of my children were baptized in the church as babies. I loved reading Bible stories and praying with them at night. Ruth and I took them to church every Sunday, and I taught in their Sunday school classes.

God gave me a purpose in my children, and I approached parenting with the same achievement focus I had with everything. I think I was striving to be Father of the Year. Not that anyone had to give me that title, I just wanted my kids to think I was.

As they grew, their different personalities shone. Brian was quiet, gentle, and had an intellectual mind—but he also had a stubborn streak. We loved reading Hardy Boys books together. Benny, whom I affectionately called "my buddy," was a chatterbox. He was competitive like me and tactile. He would run his hands through my hair and stroke his yellow blanket while I read him bedtime stories. Becca was quiet like Brian, and a sweet and gentle girl. I called her "squirt," and I carried her so much when she was little that she learned to walk late.

I was close with all three of my children, but Benny and I had something special. Maybe it was because he was the most like me. He and I would take on the first-grade boys in basketball, and he was thrilled when I lifted him up to slam dunk the basketball on the nine-foot hoop. He loved it when I came to school and had lunch with him before helping with class parties. Sometimes I took him out of school early so we could play Putt-Putt golf at our favorite course, called Parkland Putters.

Because sports had been so important to me, I wanted my kids to participate too. I wanted them to experience teamwork and sportsmanship and to build their self-esteem. I coached them in T-ball, baseball, soccer, basketball, flag football, and swimming. Where my father had been absent, I was determined to be present. I also knew the importance of teaching the commitment to do their best in school, but I was determined to accomplish this without the intimidation and humiliation Mother had imposed on me. I prayed that they would do well in school and be awarded college scholarships. What could make a dad prouder? For the first time, I could fully appreciate my mother's desire for her sons to be achievers. I just planned to go about it in a different way.

My most special Father's Day was when Brian and Benny gifted me handmade, oversize construction-paper cards with paint-stamped footprints. They'd dipped their little feet in bright white paint and left imprints of tiny toes all over the black paper. Inside, the card read, "I want to follow in your footsteps." I choked up.

"Thanks, boys," I said, ruffling their hair.

I wanted to be the kind of dad whose footsteps they would want to follow. I still struggled with some resentment toward my own dad. Seeing the innocence in my boys' eyes kept me bound to bitterness toward my dad for not being there to protect me.

Then the day came that Brian brought home the Cub Scouts flyer. Benny wasn't old enough to join yet, but I included him as if he were. Brian had the same begging excitement I'd had at his age, and Benny mimicked him in everything he did. Two brothers repeating history. The same words that had come out of my dad's mouth came out of mine: "So, you want to join Cub Scouts?" I wanted my boys to feel as important as I had when my dad left a decision like that up to me. I wanted to relay the same interest my dad had that day.

Some might wonder why I would let my boys do Boy Scouts after the abuse I endured at the hands of my Boy Scout leader. I still saw the value in the program, still had pride in having earned my Eagle Scout. Besides, there would be no place for a Bruce to weasel into their lives because I would be watching. I vowed to protect my sons by immersing myself in all the activities they would be involved in. I was just as proud to wear the uniform of Cubmaster as I had been to put on my Cub Scout uniform that first day all those years ago. Brian and Benny seemed to feel the same. Hanging on my every word, their eyes gleamed as they stood up taller on the day of our first pack meeting. I taught them the Cub Scout salute and handshake and showed them how to form their fingers into the Cub Scout sign, the wolf ears. In unison, they followed my lead. Memories of Bruce teaching me these same rituals surfaced, but I stuffed them down. This was my do-over; this was how it should have been. I told my sons, "I promise, boys, that I will take you all the way to Eagle Scout."

I may have been determined to protect my sons, but it wasn't the Boy Scouts I should have been worried about. As it turned out, there were some things I couldn't protect my children from.

Chapter 18

Broken and Blended

I NEVER IMAGINED IN A million years that a divorce trial would be one of the trials I would have to face. Blinded by daddy bliss, my wedded bliss had been slowly dissolving. I assumed children were supposed to enrich a marriage, but after fifteen years of marriage, Ruth served me divorce papers. She tried to reason with me, as if I were supposed to understand. "We are going in different directions," she said. I wasn't quite sure which direction she meant by that.

Since I was the man, I was the one who was ordered to move out. Unfortunately, that's usually how it went—no matter how great of a dad I was. It probably didn't help that Ruth claimed in the divorce papers that I was capable of making anthrax to harm our family because I was a chemical engineer at Boeing.

Driving away with only a suitcase and having to leave my three miracles behind was the most excruciating loss I had ever felt. I couldn't even bear to look in the rearview mirror. I questioned myself. *Did I let my kids take the place of where my wife should have been? Was I trying to recoup my childhood through them, knowing Bruce wasn't around to taint it this time?* I remembered Dad's warning long ago about not marrying someone like Mother. I hadn't, but I'd still been hurt. I was learning the hard way that the quiet type can be just as hurtful.

Broken down to nothing, I unlocked the door to a cold and empty apartment. My pain filled every square foot of that tiny space. That first night, I crawled into my sleeping bag in the middle of the hard floor and wept over the loss of my children, the tears soaking my pillow. I had never felt so much loss. I wanted to wail in sheer grief over them, but the walls were thin, and I didn't want my new neighbors to hear me.

All I wanted was to sleep away my troubles. But as soon as I dozed off, the angry voice of Bruce jolted my eyes wide open. I struggled to free myself from the hold of the sleeping bag. The zipper broke as I bolted up in a panic to run away from him. I came to a dead stop by running into the wall. I dropped to my knees and began to weep again. My nightmares had returned.

But the real nightmare was just beginning. The long, drawn-out twelve days between visitations with my children were wrenching. It was like being stuck in solitary confinement. The little bit of dwindled-down daddy time I was given was like tossing scraps to a starving man. My children weren't faring much better. Brian was now fourteen, an age where a boy needs a father more than ever. Twelve-year-old Benny was loyal to me to a fault, so when Ruth brought home a new boyfriend, he didn't take it well. I took them to Boy Scouts and made the most of our weekend visitations, playing foosball and making new memories, trying to keep our connection. But it wasn't enough.

Becca was still young, so I called up her day care to find out about their fees in the event that I got joint custody of the children. During our conversation, the kind woman on the phone, who knew Ruth, supplied a startling revelation.

"Your wife told me that she was kidnapped by her dad when she was three years old!"

I was horrified because Ruth had never mentioned that fact to me. It couldn't have been coincidence that Becca had been three when she served me divorce papers. Something had changed after Becca had been born. Now, everything made more sense. It became clear that Ruth was reliving her traumatic childhood through Becca and that somehow, she had twisted me into the figure of the father she feared.

One Friday night not long after the divorce, I stopped by Ruth's house to pick up the kids for my weekend. I was excited to take them for a campout on the living room floor of my apartment. I knocked on the door of what used to be my house and waited on the step until

Ruth appeared. I looked over her shoulder. No sign of Brian, Benny, and Becca. That's when I knew something was off. It was obvious this was not going to be the typical exchange that our parenting plan had designated.

Instead, Ruth handed me a thick envelope. I pulled out a stapled stack of devastation—a domestic violence order of protection. Then she shut the door, leaving me in silence on the doorstep. The little bit of life left in me extinguished. A blunt, wide-open wound in my gut couldn't have been more painful. This meant CPS—Child Protective Services—was investigating. To my total surprise, the paperwork alleged that I had molested my daughter. Rage and betrayal rippled through me. *This is not true! How could she say this?* Where had this come from? Was it a far-fetched custody tactic? This was just wrong. I would never in a million years have imposed on my children what happened to me. But Ruth claimed that it was *because* of my abuse and traumatic childhood that I had molested Becca.

I don't remember getting back into my car or driving home. All I know is I walked into my apartment alone. There would be no campout tonight.

Friday nights came and went without my children. One night, I headed for home with a box of leftovers from my party-of-one dinner out. Thirty days had passed since my life had been turned upside down, and I was still waiting to hear something about the status of my case. As the investigation ran its course, I did a lot of praying—more praying than I had ever done before. My faith told me that God would reveal my innocence, so I wasn't worried. It was not seeing my children that was torture.

When I got home, I checked my mail. There was one letter waiting in the slot. I slid it out and read the return address: Child Protective Services. *Well, this is it.* I put my box of food down and tore open the envelope. Shooting up a quick prayer, I unfolded it and skimmed down to the bottom to find the outcome of my fate. There it was. "Unfounded." Never had I imagined a word could mean so much. I sat down right there on the cement and broke into tears. I couldn't believe it. *Thank you, Lord.* Not only for the verdict, but how God was using this trial to shed light on what was still in the dark for me. I got some much-needed sleep that night.

Just like divorce didn't agree with me, being single and alone didn't either, so I leaped into a rebound relationship in record time. Rachel was a blue-eyed blonde who taught in the same Sunday school class as me. One day, she flaunted her empty ring finger in front of my face. It took me long enough to wake up and realize she wanted me to know she was available. I was so mired in my own chaos that her flirty gesture didn't register. I'd been thrown to the curb so many times that I deliberately ignored any signs of what could have been a pickup line.

I don't know if she knew all that would come with marrying me, but just one month after my divorce was final, she married me anyway.

Rebound or not, Rachel saved my life. At a time when I was low, she brought light into my life. With three children of her own, we now faced the challenge of blending our families. Despite the ups and downs of step relations and various personalities, her children were a blessing. They filled my place as a father when I couldn't be a full-time daddy to my own children anymore. I tried to fulfill what they were missing too, but there was tremendous guilt on my part in doing so, as mine were now the ones who were missing out. In turn, Rachel went to bat for me, fighting for me to see Becca during the CPS investigation and afterward. She was a wonderful stepmom to my children.

I hadn't told Rachel about my past abuse, but she got an introduction to my demons early on since our new living arrangements disrupted my sleep routine. One early morning, I was struggling with Bruce in a nightmare when my alarm clock sounded. I swung a punch to get Bruce's choke hold off me, but my punch was actually my fist banging down on the clock to shut off the snooze button. Still deep in my nightmare, I flung myself out of bed, tripped, and hit the corner of the nightstand, slicing my side open. The pain jarred me awake, and I felt the blood trickling down my leg. The throbbing that came on felt as if I had been attacked by some wild animal. That was Rachel's introduction to what it meant to be married to me.

The resulting two-inch scar signified Bruce's continued hold on me—one more reminder that I still hadn't dealt with my past.

Chapter 19

Yesterday's Children

I WAS SITTING AT MY desk at Boeing when I felt the vibration of my cell phone in my front pocket. I stopped what I was doing and removed my earplugs. At almost the last buzz, I pulled it out to see who was calling. *My brother?* I was surprised, as we rarely talked anymore, both of us busy with our own lives. If he was calling, it had to be important.

"Hey, Matt, how are you?" I said in my usual, laid-back manner.

"That sick faggot!" he yelled, with no introduction. I jumped in my seat. He had to be ranting about Bruce. I wondered why he was so amped up.

Barely taking a breath, Matt fired away. "We are going after that pedophile."

A dark swarm of the past flash-flooded inside me. "Hold on, Matt. Give me a second."

I walked over to an empty conference room, shut the door behind me, and sat down, trying to steady myself. Why was he so angry about Bruce now? It had been years. Only in passing had Matt and I ever talked about what happened that night at the drive-in. We'd downplayed it by making a Scout's honor promise to never tell a soul. Occasionally, we'd joked about what Bruce did, using our sarcasm as a cover to make sure we stayed morally straight, just as the Scout Oath required of us. A disturbing thought suddenly occurred to me. *What if that hadn't been the only time for Matt?*

For some reason, it had never dawned on me that Bruce might have messed around with Matt again. I must have been wrong. Matt's intensity made it sound as if it were more than just that one night.

107

"Out of curiosity, Matt," I asked bluntly, "how long did Bruce do this to you?"

"Uh, Tom, really?" The cold sneer in his voice rattled me. "Don't tell me you didn't know we were both competing in the same double whammy? Your turn, my turn, your turn, my turn. Bruce thought it was such a clever game, working the two of us. Tom, you do realize he called me his prize Scout too, right? He warned me not to tell you because it would upset you."

Matt and I had always been competitive. Realization sank in. *You're pitiful, Tom.*

Matt kept on unraveling the past. "Tom, do you remember that old Polaroid camera Bruce had?"

"No, I don't recall."

"Are you serious? Don't you remember seeing the snapshot slide out and the noise it made?"

Matt was so wound up he could hardly get his next words out. "Bruce showed me the nudie pictures he snapped of you and compared them to mine."

I cringed as if my body had just taken a heavy hit. Matt was remembering stuff that I didn't, but how could I deny photographic evidence?

"Hey, I have to put you on hold for a minute," Matt said.

Stunned, I sat there with the phone in my hand. Matt's words made it obvious that my blocked brain had spared me from remembering all the details of the abuse. Amnesia? PTSD, more likely. Apparently, Matt hadn't been that lucky. His wounds were still raw and wide open to the elements. He hadn't suppressed his feelings as I had. Mine were still buried underground for the most part. Neither one of us had found a happy medium.

Matt came back on the line.

"I filed a police report on Bruce last year," he said.

A police report? I didn't know anything about that. Why hadn't he told me?

"I wanted to see Bruce held accountable for what he'd done," Matt said. "Tom, I filed the report on behalf of both of us."

Bruce's threats had kept me quiet. Matt had the gumption to do what I couldn't. I didn't know what to say. Then Matt brought up something that rattled me to my core.

"Do you realize how many more victims there must be and probably still are right now? How many more boys Bruce has rocked his jollies off with?"

I didn't even want to think about it. "So, what happened with the police report?"

"I was sure justice would be served if I got the police involved. But after a yearlong investigation, they've just closed the case. You can see why I'm so angry!"

Matt told me about how he got his hopes up when the detective who investigated the report determined that there was sufficient evidence for prosecution.

"Tom, it was validation that someone had listened to me, confirmation that Bruce's twisted sex streak would be over when he was put away. All those years that creep thought he could get away with it. I would love to tell him face-to-face how I really feel. Just wait, Mr. Child Lover. A straitjacket and padded room would be suitable for a maniac like you."

I could feel darkness gathering around Matt's words as he added, "He ought to be castrated as punishment for what he did."

My mind clouded with disgusting visual memories of Bruce, now compounded by the knowledge of Matt's abuse. Matt described what the detective had written in the report about his visit to Bruce's home. Bruce had been willing to openly discuss his history with the Scouts. He even admitted to having sex with the both of us. The findings on the police report showed Bruce had confessed to relations with a nameless boy just five years ago. How many more victims were there?

Then Bruce had proceeded to nullify his actions by saying that he had since "found God." It seemed a stretch that the detective would let him off on that. But then again, I knew how charismatic and manipulative Bruce could be. Sociopath, narcissist, psycho? Whatever Bruce was, I knew Satan had been involved and worked overtime to lure even the police into his web. The detective's report had ended with this observation: "Not once during the conversation did Bruce state or indicate that he had lost his attraction to younger boys, and it appeared that his pedophilia had not waned."

Matt's voice rose again. "It sure would have been great if he 'found God' before he went on his raping rampage with you and me, plus all the other countless boys he probably violated!"

Matt started talking about retaliation. I listened but was hesitant. Retaliation wasn't in my nature, but the power of shame and humiliation associated with that man had a way of sneaking back in. The failure of the law to prosecute gave Bruce free rein to keep doing it—leaving what he did to us acceptable. Yet Bruce's threats still held a grip on me, even as a grown man. They'd been dormant for a while, but fear flushed through me again. Would he retaliate against us for going to the police? I had my own family to protect now. I hadn't told Rachel anything about this. It was probably time.

Matt sighed. "If only I'd filed the report sooner, maybe there'd be a different outcome."

I knew Matt was beating himself up. By the time he finally went to the police to file the report, the three-year statute of limitations had lapsed, resulting in no arrest. There were no charges. No prosecution. No jail time. No consequences. No nothing for what Bruce did! A measly three-year deadline had shut the case down. It no longer had any legal significance and was concluded with a status of "cleared exceptional." The only thing the police could do was retain the information. No wonder victims of sexual abuse didn't come forward more often. To bare all, only to be turned away, added insult to injury. Bruce walked free while we paid the dues for his violation.

I heard Matt smack his fist on something. "Nobody is going to get away with threatening to kill my family while killing our childhoods in the process. A statute of limitations doesn't register with a Stewart.

We were taught to overcome limitations. I intend to keep Bruce from doing this to anyone else."

Trying to defuse the tension, I joked, "You really remind me of Mother."

Matt gave a wry laugh and then switched gears. "Have you heard what's going on with the Catholic Church?"

"Uh, only in passing," I told him. I was reluctant to admit how disconnected from society I was—too preoccupied with the upheaval and clamor of my own life.

"I just read an article titled 'Church Allowed Abuse by Priest for Years.' Tom, it felt like my own past was on that page in print. It could have been our story. Authority figures used their position to groom their victims, brainwash, and abduct the innocence of their victims."

I shuddered. How could any priest of God desecrate the Lord's name by such blasphemy? Then again, how could Scoutmasters do the same, as they had sworn to do their duty under God? The only difference between the Boy Scouts and the church was in uniform.

I sensed Matt's anger subsiding as his voice turned solemn. "When the police report started to stagnate, I began to believe that maybe Bruce's abuse was all just a figment of my imagination." He paused. "That maybe I didn't matter. Seeing the story about the priests and the Catholic Church shocked me, just like one of those heart defibrillators. It woke me up. Someone listened to them. Someone believed them!"

"So, what are you going to do now?" I asked.

"It's what *we're* going to do now," Matt said. "I've already reached out to a victims' rights attorney who specializes in child abuse. Bruce himself may be exempt, but the Boy Scouts of America are not!" Matt's voice filled with hope. "Get this, Tom—the law firm's motto is 'Yesterday's Children Saving Today's Children.'"

When Matt said those words, I felt their impact. It was as if those words came to me from God Himself, giving us the go-ahead. This wasn't about revenge or retribution. It was about protecting other little boys and changing their futures. We had to be their voice. For years,

I had trusted that my suffering had purpose, seen God turn my story for good for the saving of many lives. Maybe this would be another way He would work.

Chapter 20

The Perversion Files

THE DAY MATT AND I walked into the lawyer's office for our consultation, I wasn't sure what to expect. My first impression of Tim Kosnoff was positive. He was probably in his forties, but his premature gray made him look distinguished, not to mention the fact that he was serious, super smart, and laser focused. *This man might be the key to unlocking our past.*

Matt and I settled into leather swivel chairs at a conference table. I felt proud to be sitting there next to my brother. I admired Matt's passion and spirit for getting us this far. Without him, I'd still be sitting on my secret.

Tim pulled out a yellow legal notepad and a pen. "So, tell me what happened."

Matt started reciting from his photographic memory the extent of our abuse. His descriptions triggered my own memories of the same vulgar acts, the same obscure places, and the same vicious threats. I'd never heard Matt share his side of the story in this much detail. It could have been my recollections he spoke. What Bruce had done to me, he did to Matt. If my memories had been as vivid as his, I might not have survived long enough to be sitting here today.

"That's quite a story," Tim said, leaning back in his chair after Matt finished. "I want you to know that I believe you. I'm proud of you for coming forward. That takes a lot of courage."

I believe you. Something in my heart cracked open when he said that. My mother's words echoed in my thoughts. *You're lying, Tom!*

Tim's words wrote over the memory, replacing Mother's response. He had listened.

"Taking on the Boy Scouts is going to be difficult," Tim warned us. "It's like chopping down a sequoia tree with a pocketknife."

I smiled. *An apt analogy.*

"Nothing is too much of a challenge for a Stewart," Matt said, leaning forward. We shared a knowing glance. We had Mother to thank for that.

Tim laid out his plan before rising to escort us out. "Well, that's all I need for today. I'll be in touch once I have some news for you."

As we left the office, it felt as if healing had begun. Like the abused altar boys, someone had heard our cries. Someone had listened to us. Someone had believed us.

Twelve months of fact-finding lay ahead—homework of sorts to build our case. While I was doing research, I ran across some very damaging news archives. On May 18, 1935, *The New York Times* published an article titled "Boy Scouts' 'Red Flag List' Bars Undesirables."[3] The article disclosed that a "red flag list" was being maintained by the Boy Scouts of America of "persons regarded as undesirable influences on youth." Colonel Theodore Roosevelt told the twenty-fifth anniversary meeting of the Scouts National Council, "We want to preserve fineness. We must choose between Scouts and hoodlums."

I shook my head. So much for this red flag list. It sure didn't protect us decades later.

Digging deeper, I found another article from 1991. A *Washington Times* investigation into the Boy Scouts revealed this: "The Boy Scouts are a magnet for men who want to have sexual relations with children . . . Pedophiles join the Scouts for a simple reason: it's where the boys are."[4]

Next, I read *Scout's Honor* by Patrick Boyle, which covered the history and reality of widespread molestation in the Scouts. It was even worse than I expected. The book exposed the existence of confidential records known as the "perversion files," twenty-thousand pages of documented incidents revealing over 1,200 names of suspected and confirmed pedophiles and the abuse they committed between 1965 and 1985.[5] The compilation of those files represented the largest and most comprehensive data collection on child sexual abuse by any one organization. What the Boy Scouts did to maintain the files—hush and hide evidence of abuse—may have been comprehensive, but what the Boy Scouts failed to do—protect the boys—was incomprehensible.

The Scout environment was an ideal breeding ground for child molesters. The program started boys out young, reeled them in through obedience and submission, and coerced them through the ranks by rewarding them with praise and badges. In a less-than-effective attempt to tackle the magnitude of the problem, the Scouts implemented a much-delayed effort to protect their participants. In the late 1980s, they'd put into place a youth-protection training to screen leaders by background checks, provide extensive training, and mandate report- ing of child abuse. They also adopted a "two-deep" leadership model which was to ensure no adult was ever left alone with a child. Still, it hadn't been enough.

From what I found, the Boy Scouts had been aware they were dealing with pedophiles for almost a century but had covered up the allegations of abuse to protect their name and reputation.

Particularly, the Scouts failed by not performing background checks. I knew this firsthand, as they hadn't done one on me when I took on the role of Scoutmaster in my sons' troop. Even if back- ground checks were conducted, leaders were still given the go-ahead to start immediately—before the results came back. As an organization dependent on volunteers, especially one in which volunteer positions required a lot of time and commitment, filling the need was more pressing than due diligence.

With our case against the Scouts growing, Matt and I turned our attention to Bruce specifically and began looking for any records that might reveal his misbehavior within the Scouts. Unbelievably, he was still actively leading in the Scout program. We did obtain some damning evidence with Bruce's name on it, but one specific file we requested was mysteriously missing.

My job was to reach out to the person who should have known about the goings-on with Bruce more than anyone else—the man Bruce was assistant Scoutmaster under when I was in their troop. One weekend I paid him a visit, traveling across the state to see him, since he had moved. Our meeting turned awkward as soon as I filled him in on why I was there. He immediately told me, "Make sure you're only going after Bruce and not the Scouts." It was obvious to me he was protecting the Boy Scouts of America. I continued to question him as tactfully as I could without revealing my full motives. But from then on, his answers seemed defensive, as if protecting himself from any blame by association. I chalked up the interview as another cover-up.

We were about eight months in when Matt stopped by my house one evening.

"Hey, Rachel." Matt nodded toward her as he hung his jacket on the coat hook in the hallway.

"Hi, Matt." She looked at me and back at him. "I'll go make you guys some coffee," she said and tactfully withdrew to the kitchen. I led Matt out to the patio chairs on the back porch, where the evening air was still warm.

Matt wasted no time. "I went to see Bruce today."

I froze. "You did what? Why would you do that?" I knew Bruce still lived in the area, but this was downright daring.

Matt shrugged. "Bruce has information we need. How else was I going to get it?"

I pulled my chair up to the glass table as Rachel appeared with two steaming mugs then disappeared back into the house. As soon as she was gone, I jumped on Matt. "So, what happened?"

"Well, he's married. His wife answered the door. And he's currently unemployed." Matt took a sip of coffee. "I told him I needed some closure. He gave me a sob story about how he had a demon living inside of him, how he had a sex addiction, how he was looking for love in all the wrong places. Apparently, he even sought out psychiatric help although that was probably prompted more by the police investigation than his conscience. I didn't believe a word he said. It took every ounce of me not to give him a piece of my mind and remind him how he had no problem replenishing his so-called lack of love by stealing it from little boys like me who couldn't defend themselves."

Matt curled his lip in disgust.

"And . . . ?" I asked, sitting on the edge of my seat.

"I finally asked him if he was sorry for what he'd done. He said yes, but it wasn't sincere. He started going on about how us Stewart boys were, in his oddly old-fashioned words, 'of studly athletic form' and sulked about how short and pudgy he was. When did envy ever justify sexual abuse? And he had the gall to say it was your idea to involve me sexually."

My idea? That was news to me. I shook my head. "I can't believe he's still free." In shifting the blame, Bruce had brainwashed himself.

Together, Matt and I gained strength as we prepared for what was ahead. The attorneys could use Bruce's confession to come against the Boy Scouts' negligence. This was why we were bringing the lawsuit. I thought again about the many other boys who had suffered and continued to suffer in silence. Matt and I had made it through. Not everyone had been so lucky.

Chapter 21

Sawing the Sequoia

BEFORE WE COULD OFFICIALLY FILE the lawsuit, I had two things left that I needed to do. The first was resign from my position as Scoutmaster. It was a Monday evening when I put on my Scout uniform for the last time and walked into what would be my last troop meeting and my last day as Scoutmaster. I couldn't very well continue leading the troop while I took the Boy Scouts to court. It was an agonizing decision, but unavoidable.

I went through the motions—making announcements, awarding badges, reciting the oath. I'd done it for so many years, it was second nature. I didn't even have to think. When the evening drew to a close, I stepped up to the podium. It was time to drop the bomb. Instead of starting the closing flag ceremony, I made my farewell announcement.

"This will be my last night as your Scoutmaster," I began. A murmur rippled through the boys and the parents gathered in the back of the room. The surprise and disappointment they expressed hurt me as I knew it would. I'd told no one of the lawsuit or my plans to step down. "I regret to inform you that I am resigning from my position in this troop. This hasn't been an easy decision. First, I'd like to express my appreciation for my coleaders and for all you Scouts. It's been my privilege to serve you and serve with you."

I shifted my weight and took a deep breath. "I have a secret."

For the first time, I spoke publicly about my abuse—as tactfully and appropriately as I could. I didn't mention Bruce, but I did caution the room about the real risks of abuse in the Scouts. "Never keep a secret like mine," I told the boys I'd mentored, my sons among them.

119

"If someone is hurting you or making you uncomfortable, tell someone. I care about your safety." In closing, I left no room for debate. "I can no longer participate as a leader in an organization that does not protect boys." The room went silent as I walked out the door.

The second thing I had to do was just as awkward—tell Dad about the abuse. I'd gone to Mother all those years ago, but I'd never told him. I doubted she had either. Like Mother, the words that came out of Dad's mouth when I told him about the abuse and our upcoming court case were not the ones I wanted to hear. "I don't believe that Bruce abused you," he said. "Bruce was a nice guy!" Twenty years later, the denial hurt just as much.

Superior Court Case #03-2-37274-9 would soon be considered the first of its kind, a landmark case against the Boy Scouts of America that would open the door for more to follow. Matt called it a "David versus Goliath battle." We thought the prior year of preparation had been grueling, but it was nothing compared to what we were in for. It began with a media frenzy of news coverage when we held a press conference announcing the filing of our lawsuit.

The Boy Scouts of America were tough and promised to get tougher. They were a huge institution padded with what seemed to be indestructible armor and unlimited resources to use in their defense. We had nearly a hundred years of abuse to prove, so we needed a smoking gun to gain any leverage against them. We knew what it was—the "perversion files." We just needed to get them. But of course, the Boy Scouts weren't going to hand them over without a fight. As the Boy Scouts put hurdle after hurdle in our path, I kept telling myself, *the truth always comes out.* Truth coming out was usually the result of someone's courage. We Stewarts were ready for this storm.

The time came to submit our personal declarations, where we had to disclose the explicit details of our abuse and reveal what Bruce was capable of. I had never written down any specifics about what Bruce did to me before then. I sat at my desk, a blank sheet of graph paper lit up by the lamp. Slowly, the memories began to drain down to the paper in neatly aligned block letters. The words came easier than I expected, but my emotions had a more difficult time catching up. Battling the chaos of my stressed-out marriage, my teenage sons, and the complex dynamics of my blended family had stripped the emotion out of me, not to mention the overtime I was putting in at work to keep my depleted finances afloat. The weight of my muddled life—now tangled up with the stress of the court case—was brutal. No wonder I couldn't open my feelings. I didn't have the time or the energy.

But amid it all, I did hold on to my faith—the only thing that could sustain a life like mine. I leaned on God more than ever. As the court case dragged on, I'd drive to work early each morning before the sun came up—the only time I could be still long enough to pray for that grace in my life. One morning, bright flashing lights pulled up behind my car in the empty parking lot and interrupted my devotional time. I rolled down my window as the Boeing security officer approached.

"Is there a problem, officer?" I asked.

"Sir, it looked like you were sleeping in your car. I've seen you here in the early morning for several days. I'm sorry, but you aren't allowed to park here overnight."

I chuckled and lifted the Bible off my lap. "Oh, I was just praying and reading. I come in early."

The officer looked amused. "Ah, I see. Well, carry on then."

Carry on. That was the only way forward.

After the personal declarations came the court-ordered psychological evaluations and counseling sessions. The attorneys for the Scouts were doing what they could to prove beyond a shadow of a doubt that Matt and I had turned out just fine. Then came eight-hour-long depositions. I had the opportunity to watch Bruce's deposition on videotape. It was good I didn't attend his actual deposition; otherwise, I may not have been able to maintain my composure when I heard some of the answers he gave. I know for sure Matt couldn't have.

On the screen, Bruce walked in sporting a classy suit and tie like a real gentleman would. More like a "genital man." We needed honesty from him. Would he tell the truth because he was under oath? Much to our surprise, he did. Well, most of the truth anyway—enough to baffle skeptics on both sides of the table. Bruce had begun his sex streak sometime in the sixties. Piece by piece, he unveiled how he got away with abuse by explaining how easy it had been for a pedophile to "graze in the wide-open pastures of the Boy Scouts."

The attorney asked, "What do you know about Scout leader rules?"

"I'm really not aware of any rules that were in place that I avoided or evaded," Bruce said. "It was a different time back then, and the organization didn't seem—at least outwardly—to be thinking about how to ensure that children were not abused. They just needed the help. One of the main reasons Scoutmasters were able to abuse Scouts was the lack of parental involvement. Many parents thought of Scouting as childcare. There's a joke about BSA standing for 'Baby Sitters of America.'"

In another question, Bruce was asked, "What type of conduct by a leader should have raised concerns, even in the absence of any complaints being lodged?"

Bruce answered, "Mainly the amount of time a Scoutmaster spent alone with kids, away from sanctioned Scouting activities. Another red flag should have been the degree to which individual attention was paid to a particular boy."

Throughout the deposition, Bruce was quick to blame others. Some of his outlandish excuses about me and Matt were "It was Matt's idea to be with me" and "Tom just didn't understand and asked me to show him." No matter how far-fetched Bruce's answers were, they were enough to seal his guilt even if he believed his answers were justified. Bruce also shifted his blame onto the Scouts and even the parents. But that was exactly what we needed. We couldn't go after Bruce, but his confession about how he used the faults of the Scouts to his advantage proved our point.

When it came time for my deposition, Tim and I sat down at a long conference table across from the attorneys for the Boy Scouts. The lead lawyer, the one asking the questions, was a woman. The strategy must have been to make me feel vulnerable by having to bare all the down-and-dirty details to a woman. But it wasn't the woman I needed to worry about; it was their secret weapon—Bruce Phelps himself. I stiffened in surprise as he came through the door in the flesh and sat directly across from me in the perfect position to stare me down. He'd never been handsome, and age hadn't helped him. He was still short, plump, unkempt, and now balding.

I straightened in my chair. Their tactic of menacing me into submission by making me face my abuser wasn't going to work. I wasn't going to let it. I took a sip of water from the glass in front of me and cleared my throat, ready to answer whatever they had to throw at me. I swore to tell the truth, the whole truth, and nothing but the truth, so help me God. *So, help me, God!*

As time ticked slowly by, my answers to their questions about the man I was looking at drew me back to when he was my Scout leader. He didn't wear a beard back then, but I saw the same eyes behind those thick glasses. The longer I sat there, the more lucid the past I had with Bruce became. The tedious hours were necessary to prove his guilt, but the further we got along in the day, the more difficult it became to fire darts at him. Something strange was happening during the process, a fading of animosity in my heart. I knew with all the trauma I had gone through, there was no way I could have come out the other side intact if I had allowed anger and resentment to take over my life. As I looked at Bruce, I almost felt sorry for him. Our reason for bringing this suit was to fight against the neglect of the Scouts, not to bury Bruce. Maybe he had truly found God like he said he had. If he truly had, I prayed he wouldn't get lost again.

When the deposition portion ended, I slumped back in my chair, drained. As we wrapped up, I suddenly felt an overwhelming desire to forgive this man. I'd never thought a man like that was forgivable. But I also believed that God could do anything, and I trusted in a salvation based on grace. If He could free me, why not Bruce?

Chapter 22

The Truth
Always Comes Out

MATT AND I WERE ELATED when our subpoena to obtain the perversion files was approved by the judge. In turn, the Scouts appealed. We climbed a step higher; the Scouts appealed again. We stomped on their toes yet another step higher, and they appealed again. Tim was right. A case against the Boy Scouts was like chopping down a sequoia tree with a pocketknife. But the Boy Scouts' unrelenting legal efforts shone a bright light on their guilt. What were they hiding? Their final chance to appeal brought us straight to the top—the Washington State Supreme Court. No appeal would be allowed at this level, and we prevailed. The Scouts were ordered to release the files to our attorneys. This was huge. We had our smoking gun. The documents themselves were bare-bones proof that lurid information had been kept private internally. That damning information would have hibernated indefinitely if we hadn't come along.

The information our attorney discovered within these files was even worse than our research had led us to believe. The files included scanned documents noting actual or suspected abuse occurrences. In some cases, the accused were allowed to continue with just a warning. In other instances, when they were dismissed, the displaced men outsmarted the Scouts by packing up, moving elsewhere, and reapplying to a different troop under a different name. Sometimes the name change was as simple as switching out a middle initial. That's all it took for the abuse to continue. Even though the Boy Scouts kept a so-called red flag list, it was unclear if it was ever referenced to follow up on offenders.

The perversion files also documented how the victimized boys were hushed in order to protect the presumably good name of Scouts and revealed that accusations were quietly dismissed at the astronomical rate of one every three days. Cases of abuse in the Scouts had not been reported, investigated, or turned over to the police. Instead, the Scouts had spent more attention and care on keeping it all under wraps than on protecting the victims. The most unsettling part was that from all the pedophiles listed in the twenty-year stretch of 1965–1985, Bruce's name was nowhere to be found. How many other Bruces were out there?

~

Our lawsuit had been in court for three years and five months the night that Tim called me. He only ever called when he had news on the case. I was at home with Rachel, watching a movie.

"I need to take this," I told her. "Do you mind if we pause?"

She reached for the remote.

I flipped my cell phone open and walked into the other room. "What's the latest news, Tim?"

"Tom, the Boy Scouts have proposed a settlement," he said, laying out the terms.

I didn't like the idea of settling. But Matt and I had grown weary as the case dragged on. "What's your professional opinion? Do you think we should settle?"

"Well, if this goes to trial, it could still go either way, and that's a risk you'd take. Washington State doesn't award punitive damages. It could be tricky to convince a jury that you were defenseless and helpless, even with all the proof you have."

He had a point. Matt was six foot, seven inches tall, and I was six foot, three. Because we'd gone on to make something of our lives, our professional success and overall demeanor only supported the argument that Bruce's abuse had *not* been devastating to either of us.

"I'll talk to Matt and let you know our decision," I said, and hung up.

"Was that Tim?" Rachel called from the living room.

"Yeah." I walked back in and sank into my spot on the couch. "The Boy Scouts want to settle."

"How much?" she asked.

I told her. "But I'm not sure if we should take it."

Rachel leaned her head against the couch cushions. "I'm tired, Tom. I don't know how much more our family can take. I've hardly seen you these last three years, you've been so busy at work and wrapped up in the lawsuit. We're like ships passing in the night. I've been holding down the home front on my own."

"Look, I know it's been tough," I said. "I've been working so hard to keep everything together. You know how important this case is for me."

Rachel pulled her knees up to her chest. "Yeah. Yeah, I do. But look at what it's cost us. And I don't mean money."

I sighed. She was right. The emotional strain of this case had taken its toll on me. On us.

"So, what are you going to do?" she asked.

I headed for the door. "I'm gonna go call Matt."

✲

Rather than going into a long court battle with an unpredictable outcome, Matt and I agreed to settle out of court in 2007, ending with no trial. I was relieved, as my energy was gutted. What was left of my dysfunctional family was fragile, and it would have been detrimental to drag them through the media circus of a trial.

It was never about financial compensation. No amount of money could buy back my innocence or restore my childhood. I was there for what we actually did walk away with—the freedom to tell our story without a gag order. The settlement wasn't large by my calculation, but it covered our costs and gave me and Rachel a nice nest egg. Since we didn't go to trial, the perversion files obtained by our attorney had to be returned to the Boy Scouts, stalling them from public release—but not for long.

Miraculously, our landmark case set in motion what needed to continue. Following our out-of-court settlement, a lawsuit filed in the state of Oregon did go to trial and prevailed. Rooted in our initial discoveries, the case precipitated the Boy Scouts' greatest fear: the exposure of clear evidence showing the sexual-abuse epidemic in the Scouts. They could no longer hide behind their name. In 2012, five years after our case, the Oregon Supreme Court mandated the Boy Scouts of America to release the perversion files through 1985. A handful of other court cases followed, revealing some more recent files. However, as it stands now, the Scouts have yet to release files from 1991 to the present.

In my eyes, God's purpose for "the saving of many lives" was coming to fruition. Our goal had been to help protect those who had yet to fall victim to abuse by preventing pedophiles from joining the Scouts, bringing awareness to the problem, and encouraging other victims to come forward. Though we may not have cut down the whole sequoia, our little pocketknife had chipped away enough to allow others to fell the tree, leaving a swath of blue sky overhead. The truth had come out.

Chapter 23

Tough Love

THE SHARP RING OF THE phone woke me. I rubbed my eyes, still blurry with sleep, and looked over at the digital clock on the night-stand. 2:35 a.m. The phone rang again. I only had a couple more rings before I'd miss it, so I pushed back the covers, threw my legs over the side of the bed, and stumbled to the kitchen, grabbing the landline phone from its cradle on the wall.

"Hello?" I answered.

"Is this Mr. Stewart? Tom Stewart?"

"Yeah, that's me," I mumbled.

"This is Officer Peterson with the Tacoma police. I'm sorry to inform you that your son Brian was caught shoplifting at a local Safeway store. We're going to take him down to the station. Would you like to meet us there?"

Not again. I flicked on the light switch and squinted into the sudden brightness. "Okay, I'll be there."

I hung up the phone and leaned against the counter, rubbing my forehead. This wasn't the first call in the night I'd received. Now that the Boy Scout lawsuit was finally over, the trouble with my teenage sons had taken front and center. Every time the phone rang, I feared the worst. I'd spent many nights out searching for my prodigals. The sleep deprivation was almost as bad as when they were infants.

I slipped back into the bedroom and pulled pants and a shirt from the closet, trying not to wake Rachel. *I should just sleep in my clothes.* Grabbing my car keys, I headed out the door.

The kids had been devastated when Ruth and I divorced. Since then, the boys' rebellion had only grown. I'd tried my best to maintain my place as their dad, keeping Scouts front and center, remembering my promise to get them to Eagle Scout. But the limited time we spent together at Scouts, tied into their every-other-weekend visitation, was only a fraction of the time boys their age needed from a father's influence.

Outside peer pressure became more alluring than our father-son relationship. They began hanging out with the wrong type of friends. First it was cigarettes, then marijuana. Now the shoplifting. What would I do? Discipline was hopeless. Brian would sneak out, just to be returned home by the police after we reported his running away. He opted to couch surf at whichever friend's house had a vacancy. Attempts to ground him were a joke. His smug disrespect was getting worse.

Brian wore a familiar expression of apathy when I arrived at the police station. He didn't look at me as he gathered his things. The officer with him turned to me.

"The store won't be pressing charges—this time," he said. "Next time it might be a different story."

"Thank you," I said. Brian followed me out to the car and climbed into the front passenger seat. I slid in, turned the ignition, and pulled onto the freeway toward home. We sat in silence, until finally, I spoke.

"We can't keep doing this," I said quietly.

"Watch me," Brian retorted.

I glanced over at him. "Are you high?"

"What's it to you?"

I gripped the steering wheel. I didn't know what else to do. It was a long, silent drive home.

I thought it had been bad before, but things only got worse. The pot issue was minor compared to what was coming. Addiction was gaining—an invasion of evil that overwhelmed Brian and Benny and stole their willpower. Brian lost all interest in high school. Drugs robbed him of all motivation and dulled his genius-level IQ. He settled for a GED. Benny was an apprentice to Brian's bad choices, shadowing him as if it were a competition—just like Matt had with me. The brothers' influence on each other was way more enticing than mine. Their Scout Oath went by the wayside and then some. Benny, too, settled for a GED. Any hopes I had for them attending college or following in my footsteps were for naught. Their futures had slipped right out from underneath them. I didn't understand. My brother and I had both graduated as valedictorians. *Where had I gone wrong?*

I had to admit that my approval addiction was just as much of a problem, albeit less visible. The patterns were identical. It was either the need to feel loved or the need for drugs—seek, find, receive, regret, withdrawal . . . and repeat. In my eyes, my boys' addiction was a failure on my part, and I didn't do failure. Mother had made sure of that. My inability to control my sons' failures forced me to face my own addiction to achievement. I wanted a daddy do-over. I wished I could start my role as a father all over again.

The next couple years I rode the roller coaster of addiction with them. Thirty days detox, then back to the drugs. Six months in a rehab program, then back on the streets. No matter how many treatment programs they shuffled through, the bind of their addiction grew tighter with each go-around. When Brian contracted MRSA (a difficult-to-treat staph infection) in his arm, I was hit with the naked truth that he was shooting up heroin. It didn't take his life, but his entire forearm was riddled by disfiguring scars, proof of how close he came to death. The outward damage was bad, but it was only a fraction of what was going on inside. The next generation of Stewart brothers were wallowing through their own living hell. Different from the hell that Matt and I lived, but it was hell just the same. My mind had barricaded my pain. My boys had sought out drugs to block theirs.

Devastated to see how far my boys had drifted, Rachel and I had to learn the language of addiction. Though it became the norm for us, we fought like heck to not make it the norm for any of the other kids in the home. But it wasn't enough. Trying to survive the heartache of what had become of them consumed all I had left, leaving only bits and pieces for the rest of our blended family. My family was falling apart.

I threw myself into my work at Boeing, where I could escape from the chaos of my life. Doing what I had learned to do so well, I blocked out what was tearing up my life, got in my car, and headed off to work. I didn't know how to cope any other way. While my family imploded, I found comfort in chemical reactions I could control. I also found refuge at church, away from the rigmarole. Every Sunday morning, I'd find my way to my usual seat, front row over to the right. Unfortunately, the seats saved next to me for my family became empty. Endless prayers for my disintegrating family seemed to bounce off the walls.

My daily journal became an outlet for expressing my sadness and confusion. I penned desperate pleas of help for my sons.

God, I'm scared to death of the black hole they're approaching. I'm afraid that they'll go so far there's no way back. I wanted the bad experiences to end with me, but my boys are suffering just as much. Please, Lord, I'd take on any sacrifice to protect them. I believe you can work things for good. Why aren't you intervening? Will there be no relief?

I could hardly take it anymore, and neither could Rachel. The next phone call wasn't about Brian or Benny, but I had the same feeling of dread in my gut. I was right. It was divorce—again. After a six-week separation, she moved out and moved on with her life. I'd lost my kids to the first divorce, and now I'd lost my stepkids, whom I loved as my own. *Why does this keep happening to me?*

With the house empty of any family who might be negatively affected by Brian and Benny, I decided to let them move in with me for a while. My hope was to give them another chance to get their lives together with me right there. In my denial, I hoped their addiction wouldn't move back in with them. But my hope alone was not strong enough. It didn't take long to realize my mistake. The drugs had become good at manipulating them; in turn, they became good at manipulating me. I wasn't prepared for the appendages of the drug world that appeared under my roof. Items of value would soon start coming up missing. My house became a hazardous waste area. I never knew what I might find hiding underneath their mess. It brought back unpleasant memories of Mother's hoarding.

Fitted with industrial rubber gloves, I inspected their rooms, sifting through the mess they created for any drug paraphernalia that might have been smuggled in. I didn't want to face what I found: blackened spoons and tinfoil, pen caps, empty prescription bottles, and plastic baggies with white residue. That was hard enough. But when I heard a bright-orange-capped syringe bouncing around in the dryer, it became real. When I almost pricked my finger on a used syringe with an exposed needle, I made my choice. The boys couldn't stay.

I gave them a choice—rehab again or the streets. Brian chose the streets. Benny thankfully chose rehab, but as always, it didn't last. I had dreamed we'd be a father and son team that one day would stand up in front of hundreds of people talking about how he got free from drugs and how they could too. His arm would be visual proof for those who might be teetering toward the druggie side of life. But that hope faded with every relapse.

One morning I found Benny sleeping in his car in the driveway. He admitted he'd been kicked out of the clean-and-sober house for not staying clean and sober.

It was incredibly hard to tell him, "I'm sorry, son, you can't stay."

Doing what I had to do, I changed the locks on the house. I never knew what was coming next or what to expect, and I had to put my foot down, restricting them from coming near the property completely. Tough love was as tough on me as it was on them.

Chapter 24

Wings

I WIPED THE SWEAT FROM my forehead as the hot August sun climbed higher in the sky. I'd started on yard work early this Saturday, trying to beat the heat. I'd climbed the hill up to the barn on my property with the weed eater in tow. My earplugs muffled its steady drone as the vibrations rippled through my body. It felt good to get outside after a long week of working out calculations and chemicals at Boeing. The weed eater left a swath of shorn weeds and instant gratification. The menial labor provided me an escape, blocking out the troubles of my life. Mother had taught me how to fake "okay" so well, that at times, I could pretend my life was okay.

The weed eater sputtered, telling me it was running out of gas, so I shut off the motor to refill it. As I did, a car pulling off on the side of the road caught my eye. It braked, coasting toward where I stood in the field. I was surprised to see Benny get out of the passenger seat. He was with a friend whom I hadn't met before. His big, bright smile lit up his face as he came toward me. I pulled out my earplugs and welcomed him with a hug, feeling a mixture of excitement to see him and sadness about his situation.

"I was hoping you would be home, Dad," he said. "I wanted to stop by really quick and tell you something." His words were as sincere as I had ever heard. He looked happy. "Dad, I don't know what I ever would have done without you. I would be dead without you. Thank you for putting your foot down. I'm going back into treatment."

I was speechless, his words melting some of the sadness in my heart. When tears sprang up in his eyes, emotion rose in my chest.

"I love you, and I'm so proud of you," I said, pulling him into another embrace and squeezing him tightly, like a child hugging a favorite teddy bear. For a moment, he was my buddy again, my little boy. I could pretend for at least a little while that the divorce had never happened, that drugs had never come and kidnapped my son. I savored the moment.

Benny pulled back and looked toward the car. "I have to go. I'll call you, okay?"

As I watched him leave, I blinked away my tears. I wanted to run after him, but instead, I trudged up to the barn, refilled the gas tank of the weed eater, and sat in the pebbled dirt in the shadow of the barn. Part of me wanted to rescue him again, to keep him home with me. But I knew I had to let him go. I'd had a glimmer of hope after Benny's stint in the Salvation Army Rehabilitation Center, followed by the chance to change his life in Job Corps. He'd even obtained his high school diploma. Maybe this time rehab would stick. I wanted to believe that this time would be different.

The worry of a father never ends. I hadn't heard from Brian at all recently. The hardest thing for me to do was to not cave in when he did call. That's what I did best—cave in. All my life I'd tried to please the people around me. But with the boys, I had to stick to my guns when they were angry with me. It was a constant battle as a parent, a broken parent at that.

At church the next day, the pastor preached a sermon where he shared about the chaplain side of his job. He said the hardest part was having to tell parents their child wasn't coming home. When he talked about how many doors he had knocked on to tell parents their kids had overdosed and didn't make it, I could feel the shiver through my bones. That was my greatest fear, knowing that my own sons were living on the wild side, walking on that edge. I couldn't fathom what those parents must go through and what it must be like for him to deliver that kind of devastation. I watched as his face dropped when he said, "You don't ever want me to be knocking on your door in my chaplain's uniform." I shut my eyes, my heart throbbing. I was thankful that a knock like that had not come to my door.

Sunday night, I lay awake thinking about the sermon. All the way to work Monday morning, I couldn't disconnect from the somber thoughts weighing on me. The whole day dragged. I called Benny on my lunch break, and when he didn't answer, I left a short message, hanging up with "Love you, Benny." That afternoon, I worked out on the warehouse floor rather than in the office. My coworkers hadn't been too friendly ever since I'd solicited donations for the Adopt-A-Family Christmas program. These days, I chose to work out on the floor to avoid the office tensions.

I worked late that day. Most everyone else had gone home for the evening, with the exception of a few other engineers. Sitting in the quiet, I kept looking over at my phone, feeling as if it were trying to get my attention. I was startled when it rang. The buzz seemed louder than normal. Maybe it was Benny.

I looked over at the screen. The number was withheld. I pushed the talk button and cautiously said, "Hello?"

A deep, serious male voice asked, "Is this Mr. Thomas Stewart?"

"Yes, it is," I said.

A pause.

"Uh, Mr. Stewart, this is the Black Diamond Police Department."

I was so used to getting calls from the police about the boys, I responded with "Okay, which Stewart would it be this time?" I even added a slight chuckle.

I heard him clear his throat. "Mr. Stewart, I am calling about your son, Benjamin. Your son is Ben Stewart, correct?"

I nodded as if he could see me through the phone. The conversation was odd. I'd never heard such a flat tone in a voice like that before.

"Mr. Stewart, I am deeply sorry to inform you that your son is deceased."

I stopped breathing.

I couldn't swallow, couldn't move.

I heard him say "drug overdose" before the phone fell to the floor. I didn't want to pick it up. I didn't want to hear any more.

I didn't need to hear what happened. I had prepared my heart long ago for the inevitable. I knew the odds were stacked against two people so addicted to drugs. Finally, I bent over to grab the device that had been the bearer of so much bad news. I vaguely listened to where my son had been taken, then hung up before his goodbye. For twelve years, the phone had been my compass, telling me where I needed to go to rescue my boys. I'd jump up, hop in my car wearing my hero cape, and go save them.

But now, Benny was dead. I couldn't rescue him this time. My tears came fast and heavy. I slumped over my desk, numb, and burrowed my head into my arms. I was grateful that no one on the warehouse floor was around to see me. Behind my eyes, a surreal picture of Benny's face smiled so brightly—like when he'd come to see me on Saturday. The last day I would ever see him. The last hug I would ever get from my buddy. *Thank you, Lord, that I was standing on that hill.* What was I going to do without him?

The rest of the week was a blur. I didn't go to the viewing before his funeral. It was probably best that I didn't. My pastor was gracious enough to do that for me. I wanted to remember Benny's smiling face from the last day I saw him. From the coroner's report, we learned the time of Benny's death was estimated at 1:00 p.m. He was found dead in the guest bedroom of his friend's home of an accidental overdose (pharmaceutical morphine and oxycodone intoxication). The time of his death resonated with me. It was the same time I left my phone message for him. I had sensed something strange that day when he didn't pick up his phone or call me back. I had a strong feeling that was not just a coincidence.

At his funeral, it was standing room only—evidence of what Benny's life had meant to others. All the dysfunctional relationships of my life were awkwardly joined together that day to mourn my son. When I walked into the church, the first thing I noticed was all the flowers sent in memory of him, full of color and life, just like Benny.

To one side of the stage was an easel with a whimsical, hand-painted portrait displaying my son's dynamic face. I'm not sure how I made it through the service. Becca sang a song about how she missed her brother, and the picture slideshow cracked me open. Through the haze of my tears, I saw him come back to life for a while, my world as his daddy revealed in one heartbreaking photo after another, fading out to the last picture taken by my side on what had been his last birthday.

When it was my turn to speak, I shared what it was like to be Benny's dad and how grateful I was for the twenty-three years I had with him. It was easier than talking about the years ahead I wouldn't have. Benny's heart had always been to help those trapped in addiction, even though he couldn't get free himself. I was now one of those grieving parents that the chaplain had talked about.

I also told a few quirky stories about him to lighten the mood. My favorite was this: When Benny was two, he came along on a drive with a close friend of mine named Larry. Benny had always been overly protective of me, and during the entire three-hour car ride, every time Larry and I would try to talk, Benny interrupted Larry from the backseat by repeating, "No, Larry . . . No!" As tickled as Larry was, when he stepped out of the car, laughing, he said, "I don't ever want to hear my name again!"

After the service, we released helium balloons filled with personal messages. All that I wanted to say wouldn't fit on that little note of paper. This is what I did write: "I love you, Benny, my buddy." Watching my balloon float away, I took the phrase used at his funeral as my own and told him, "It's not goodbye; it's 'See you soon!'"

We chose to have Benny's body cremated. I put a small portion of Benny's ashes in a vial around my neck with an eagle emblem dangling from the chain; he had earned his Eagle Scout after all. The rest I put in a black box embellished with an eagle and the verse:

> He gives strength to the weary and increases the power of the weak. Even youths grow tired and weary, and young men stumble and fall; but those who hope in the Lord will renew their strength. They will soar on wings like eagles;

they will run and not grow weary, they will walk and not
be faint. (Isaiah 40:29–31 NIV)

In the months after Benny's death, I clung to the memory of
his last hug. It quenched some of my grief. I also grappled with God,
slowly coming to grips with His purpose in this tragedy. How could
I see God's goodness in my son's death? Once the shock and initial
wave of grief passed, I could see how God had saved Benny from his
addiction. Benny was no longer a slave to the evil of drugs. He was no
longer suffering. The recovery houses had not been enough, and my
house had not been enough—the Lord's house was where he needed
to be. My sorrow eased a little, knowing Benny was finally sober and
safe at his forever home in heaven.

Sometime after Benny's death, I ran into the mother of one of
his friends. She urgently pulled me aside. "Tom, I have to tell you. My
son was addicted to heroin. But the night of Benny's funeral, he was
supernaturally healed from his addiction. He's been sober ever since."
Chills ran down my arms. It wouldn't be the last time. In the coming
days, others specifically sought me out to tell me my son's death was
not wasted. At least two of Benny's friends stopped using drugs altogether because of him. And it wasn't just his friends who were affected
by his life and death—Benny's death was eventually the catalyst that
enabled Brian to get out of the drug world. It was meaningful to me
if his death saved even one life.

I had always prayed that God would use my story for the saving
of many lives. Now He was using Benny's.

Chapter 25

One Step
of Forgiveness

ON THE MORNING OF DECEMBER 31, 2015, I sat in my den pondering the last fifty-three years of my life. Swiveling in my black leather armchair, I leaned forward and gazed at the pictures of my children that hung on the wall. Benny's smiling face looked back at me as a young boy. It had been a year and four and a half months since his death, and no—time had not made it any easier. Did these memories help me get through, or did they keep me shackled to my heartache? I still missed him terribly.

I looked down at my watch and did a double take. 8:11 a.m. Benny had died on that day—August 11, the eighth month and the eleventh day. Ever since his death, God had started speaking to me through numbers. Correlations of numbers that crossed my path— whether it be on a clock, my watch, my cell phone, or a page I turned to in a book—relayed a sign to me. Leaning back in my chair, I waited for what might come next. Then He spoke. The date was 12/31/2015. The numbers in 2015 added up to 8—the month Benny died. The two ones in 12/31 were for 11—the day he died. The remaining 2 and 3 signified his age—23—when he died. To me, it was a clear sign like no other, a message straight from God about Benny. It had to be. I closed my eyes, hoping to see his face.

But it wasn't Benny's face that popped into my mind. Someone else's did—a face I didn't want to see. Then, a revelation came to me as clear as the face I saw. God had got my attention through Benny's numbers, but the message was about someone else, a nudge to take the next step on my journey of forgiveness. *Go see Bruce.*

This wasn't totally out of the blue. I'd been meeting with a good friend of mine, Dean Smith, of Live to Forgive Ministries. Dean had forgiven his stepfather, Bob, for taking the life of his mother. I'd read what the Bible said about forgiveness, but Dean's words resonated with me. I knew if he could forgive his stepfather for doing something so horrific, I needed to listen. Dean said, "Forgiveness is the gateway to experiencing the best life God has for me. Through His love, my focus was redirected from my tragedy to His awesome grace. Get honest with God about the 'Bobs' in your life."

My "Bob" was Bruce.

I'd let go of my resentment toward Bruce during the lawsuit and taken the first steps of forgiveness then. But the nightmares still haunted me, and the pain of my past wasn't fully healed or resolved. I knew I had a choice to either continue to bury the pain or work toward healing. Burying the pain hadn't worked for me. It was clear God knew better and had gently nudged me to do something about it.

I knew Bruce's address, so I looked up directions. The drive would take about fifty minutes. It was going to take me at least that long to formulate the words I needed to say. I felt my courage rising. Everything I had gone through in the past had conditioned me; the hard times building my strength like workouts at a fitness club. I may have started out weak, but as each incident happened, my endurance grew. The entire way there, I tried to come up with what to say, but nothing came to mind. What was there to say anyway?

After exiting the freeway, it got real. My heart quickened and then pounded in my chest. I pulled over and parked on the side of the road and asked myself, *Are you emotionally up for this?* I took a sip of water, then gagged as my stomach tried to send it back up. Adrenaline intensified in my body. *Why am I doing this?* I didn't take long to answer myself. *Because, dummy, God told you to.*

Gathering up my confidence, I pulled back out on the road, pretending that Benny was sitting in my passenger seat as my navigator.

I took the right-hand turn and said out loud, "This is it. This is the road," as if Benny really were sitting next to me. I slowed to nearly an idle, scanning the houses for the right number. When I saw it on my left, I stiffened. I parked down the street, out of the line of sight but where the house was still visible from my side mirror. *You didn't come all this way to hide out*, I told myself as I opened the door and stepped out, determined to see this through. I wrapped my hand around Benny's vial hanging from my neck. As I walked, I felt stronger and less nervous with each step.

I was caught off guard by an unfamiliar man who came out of Bruce's house. From the sidewalk, I casually asked him if he knew Bruce.

"I'm his brother-in-law," he said, then led me right up to the front door. Cracking it open, he called out, "Hey, there is someone here to see you."

My pulse raced as I heard footsteps from inside the house coming toward me. Then he was standing there in the doorway—Bruce himself. He had a look of incredulity on his face. His brother-in-law started to introduce me, but Bruce cleared his throat and interrupted with a dry "Yeah, I know who he is." He didn't extend his hand to shake mine, and his expression was not welcoming.

This was a huge mistake. I didn't know why I expected anything else.

Bruce opened the door the rest of the way and stepped outside as his brother-in-law excused himself. Thirty-five years had gone by since the last time he and I had been alone together. I hadn't seen him since the lawsuit deposition.

We made awkward small talk at first. His manner was withdrawn and his voice low, his demeanor as if nothing bad had ever happened between us. I couldn't tell if there was any remorse in his subdued mannerisms. But I wasn't there to chat or shoot the breeze. I didn't wait long for a break to say what I needed to. "Bruce, I'm here because I want to tell you face-to-face that I forgive you for what happened."

Silence.

I remembered his claim of finding God. I hoped and prayed that was still true. But the hostile look on his face said otherwise. Instead, it sent the clear invitation to leave. I didn't expect him to shake hands goodbye, and he didn't. As I walked away, the words he shot out shook me. "I hope this means you and Matt are done lying about all of this." I looked back, and he turned and walked away.

I wasn't expecting some miraculous apology from Bruce. That's not what this visit was for. I was shaking when I got into my car, but as I started to drive home, I felt calmer. The fear in my head was gone. I had just survived a crash course in forgiveness—the reason I had gone there in the first place. For thirty-five years, I hadn't been able to fully forgive Bruce. Now, an incredible peace settled over me, a release.

My friend Dean had also told me, "One step of forgiveness can lead to a lifetime of blessings."

The day I extended forgiveness to Bruce, I walked away with some of those blessings Dean spoke of, starting with a renewed heart.

Chapter 26

Soaring

FORGIVENESS WAS JUST THE FIRST step in my journey to healing. Forgiving Bruce and my mother didn't undo the past or fix my present broken reality. Benny was still gone, and I still faced the fallout from damaged relationships. In the wake of a third broken marriage, I found a room to rent in Everett, Washington, near my job at Boeing—one of the few things that had remained constant in my life. While my circumstances may have still been difficult, God was at work.

I believe with all my heart that God takes us back through doorways of pain in order to set us free from past trauma. When my landlady in Everett had to move, she invited me to come with her to her new house, but she didn't have a room for me initially. "Would you mind sleeping in the basement?" she asked. "I could put up a tent temporarily for privacy." Oh, the irony. She couldn't have known how many times I'd been abused in my parent's basement or in Bruce's tent. Yet I agreed.

My first night in the basement, I went through my routine. For the last thirty-eighty years, bedtime had been something I didn't even want to think about. Every night was like preparing myself to walk into a danger zone. Following a strict routine was the only thing that gave me enough strength to get into bed. My nightly regimen began with shutting all doors, as if I were attempting to keep Bruce's evil locked out. I would turn on a large, noisy fan next to my bed to drown out any sudden noises that could remind me of Bruce's approach. Earplugs were my reinforcements to make sure no noise cut through.

Otherwise, Bruce's voice might wake me or prevent me from falling asleep altogether.

My digital alarm clock had to be turned the other way so I couldn't see the large red numbers. Watching each minute tick by took me back to Bruce's bedroom where time stood still until he was done. Counting the minutes turned into counting hours if I gazed at it long enough. With my eye mask slung over my forearm, I would make sure not to bend over and crawl into bed like normal people do. I was too paranoid that Bruce might secretly be hovering behind me, ready to pounce. Instead, I backed up to the bed until I felt the mattress against my legs, enabling me to sit down and inch my way under the covers. I wrapped myself into my heavy comforter, tucked in and tightly swaddled. I felt it would keep him from getting close to me, just in case he snuck into my room late at night through the window. I desperately sought sleep but dreaded when the dreams might hit.

It was a daunting routine, but necessary to keep my triggers at bay—triggers that tonight I couldn't avoid. God had brought me into a situation which simulated my childhood, where I had to face the fears I'd been managing since I was eighteen years old. But in doing so, He set me free of thirty-eight years of nightmares. Only God could do that kind of miracle.

A year later, I left the tent in the basement to move into a room on a third-floor apartment. As soon as I walked into the apartment, it was apparent that the landlady—also a Christian—was a hoarder. Having grown up in the home of a hoarder, I knew only God would lead me back into this situation. She led me through stacks of knickknacks and newspapers to show me the room, making small talk. On top of one of the piles lay a Boy Scout handbook. She picked it up and turned to me. Out of the blue, she said, "I'm concerned about the safety of my son when he goes into Boy Scouts. Do you know anything about pedophiles in the Boy Scouts?"

I tried to keep my jaw from going slack. She didn't know anything about my history or the lawsuit Matt and I had brought against the Boy Scouts. Talk about a life-changing, burning-bush moment! That

Boy Scout handbook might as well have been on fire. Only God could have orchestrated a moment like that.

"Well, as a matter of fact, I do," I said.

She opened the secondhand Boy Scout handbook, and I got a glimpse inside the cover. There was a date inscribed—the date the manual's previous owner had joined the Boy Scouts: 3/18/07. Another divine number. Benny's birthday was 3/18, and my childhood home address was 1807 Austin Road. Needless to say, I obeyed God and took the room. I found myself saying "Only God" a lot over the next couple years as I watched Him work in my life.

When a coworker invited me to attend New Life Foursquare Church, I jumped at the opportunity to plug in to a church again. It anchored me during this season of floating adrift, searching for purpose and meaning. Each Sunday, I brought my brokenness before God, leaning on Him to pick up the pieces of my life.

One Sunday, the man sitting in the row in front of me turned around and introduced himself after the service.

"I'm Vince," he said, sticking out his hand.

I shook it. In the course of our conversation, I learned that Vince had also recently gone through a nasty divorce and had been a prison guard at the Monroe Correction Complex, which was about half an hour from Everett. A balding man in his seventies, Vince didn't look like a prison guard. Although he was nearly as tall as me, he had a slender frame and the gentleness of a grandpa.

"Would you ever be interested in volunteering for prison ministry?" he asked after I shared a bit of my story. "I'm part of a ministry called Bridges to Life."

"Sure," I said. Maybe this would give me something to do, something to focus on besides my struggles. "Tell me more about it."

Vince nodded. "Bridges to Life is a volunteer-led restorative justice program that centers on responsibility, repentance, and restitution. They operate in prisons all over the country. As a volunteer, you meet weekly with the inmates and guide them through the BTL curriculum. Each session is fourteen weeks."

The number leaped out at me, as so many others had since Benny's death. Fourteen? Benny had died in 2014. Was this another nudge from the Holy Spirit?

Vince went on. "The program looks for volunteers who have been affected by crime, and they are asked to share their story with the inmates. This way, the offenders hear how criminal actions affect not only the victims, but the friends and families of those victims and society at large."

I thought of Matt and the Boy Scouts. Yep, I had a story to share.

Vince ran his fingers through his hair. "I've seen firsthand the difference this program makes for inmates. The victim-impact approach sparks empathy in offenders, the first step to accepting responsibility for their actions."

"Yeah, that sounds powerful," I said. "How do I sign up?"

He fished out a business card. "Call this number and talk to Judy. She's the BTL ministry leader. They're starting a new session soon."

I thanked him and headed for the parking lot with a new friend and a new mission.

The first day of my first session with BTL, I pulled into the parking lot at Monroe Prison. It looked like what you'd expect a prison to look like—plain, ugly, cream-colored walls surrounded by tall chainlink fences topped with rolls of barbed wire. A watchtower looked out over the grounds. I'd been assigned to the Twin Rivers Unit, which housed mainly sex offenders. I knew that was no coincidence.

I found my fellow volunteers and we entered together, passing through one metal detector, a series of doors, and then another metal detector. Inside was just as bleak as outside. Industrial gray cement floors reflected harsh fluorescent lights as we passed a row of cells with small, barred windows in each door. The air felt dense, constricting, the same way it had in the basement with Bruce. I'd been in bondage to Bruce, and I'd been imprisoned in the home of a hoarder. This, *here*, was the manifestation of everything that represented.

Once we passed into the main prison building, the warden led us to a large room with about seventy chairs circled in seven groups of ten.

I settled into one, and soon the room swarmed with tan uniforms. The seats in my circle filled, and I introduced myself. Part of the program involved each prisoner sharing their personal story, so we began there. The stories that came out in that first week and in the weeks that followed broke my heart.

Most of the inmates had been beaten or abandoned by their parents. One shared that his mother had been a prostitute and his father a drug dealer. *What kind of chance did a boy stand with parents like that?* Another inmate shared how his father had whipped him until he nearly died from excessive bleeding. He'd gone to prison for later killing his father. But the one that got to me was the man who hadn't been able to attend his child's funeral because he was in prison. I understood his grief. The pain of losing Benny still throbbed. I couldn't imagine not getting to say goodbye.

As I developed relationships with the men in my group, I came to see them with new eyes. I'd had a brutal childhood, but it didn't even begin to compare to theirs. Their stories gave me a new lens for my own past pain and an empathy for their situation. I couldn't judge them for their crimes. If I'd lived their childhoods, I'd probably be in prison too. If there were a prison for pride, I'd be on death row! I'd come into prison ministry hoping that my story would be a blessing to the inmates, but as it turned out, their stories were impacting me.

Week nine of the program focused on forgiveness, and that week I had the opportunity to share my testimony with three different units in the prison, including the Twin Rivers sex offenders. I looked out at a room full of Bruces and I told my story. I looked them in the eyes and told them about the abuse, about the Boy Scouts, about Benny—everything. Over the years, by God's grace, the silence that Bruce had held me to with his gun had grown into courage to speak out. It had started with the lawsuit, and now I'd come full circle. God yet again was using my suffering for good, for the saving of many lives.

"You can't change the past," I said. "But God can change your future. Make the most of your time in prison to draw close to Him. Only He can bring healing."

Afterward, a man named Bob approached me with tears in his eyes. "The story of your abuse had me in tears, but when you showed us the vial around your neck with Benny's ashes, I completely lost it." He blew into a handkerchief. "I have been through many programs here in the prison, but your story is the one that broke me. Anyone who doesn't believe in God before hearing your story will believe in God after hearing it. Your story will touch the heart of everyone who hears it. If you can forgive your Boy Scout leader of horrific sexual abuse through the power of the Holy Spirit, then I can certainly forgive anyone in my life who has harmed me."

I put a hand on his shoulder, wiping my own tears away.

Rick Warren says in his book *The Purpose Driven Life* that your greatest ministry comes from your greatest pain. The Lord has delivered me from the emotional damage of my afflictions and has redeemed them, using them for His good by equipping me to help free other victims who are still held captive by the chains of their past. The difficult circumstances I faced cultivated the compassion I needed to help others. I've learned how to understand the weary, the weak, and the faint because I've been one of them. It is now one of my life missions to speak out against the devastating effects of divorce and drug addiction. I can also minister to couples who have lost a child. Throughout my trials, God has helped me in my weakness, increased my endurance, and given me strength and resilience.

I've learned that submitting my will to His is not weakness—it's pure courage! Nothing is more powerful than that. My purpose in life is to be an advocate for how trusting in God can sustain us through life's trials. I want to encourage those experiencing abuse not to allow the bitterness and the evil that it came from to consume them, but to overcome as victors instead of victims. I want to encourage those who are broken to persevere, to help them rise up on wings like eagles.

Epilogue

ON FEBRUARY 18, 2020, THE Boy Scouts of America filed for Chapter 11 bankruptcy, in part because of the mounting costs of a cascade of lawsuits over abuse claims. Over the last several years, the BSA's financial woes forced them to sell many of their camp properties, including Camp Kilworth outside of Dash Point, Washington.

By November 2020, over 92,700 claims of sexual abuse had been made by former Scouts. Some are suing the organization for the release of all the "perversion files," which supposedly contain the names of 7,819 men who abused boys under their charge, along with 12,254 victims.

While survivors will now have to pursue their claims in bankruptcy court rather than via civil proceedings, according to the BSA national chair Jim Turley, the bankruptcy filing will benefit victims by allowing the organization to "equitably compensate all the victims of abuse." BSA voluntarily created a compensation trust and ran advertisements encouraging victims to come forward. "The BSA cannot undo what happened to you, but we are committed to supporting you and to doing everything in our power to prevent it from happening to others," Turley wrote.

A statement from the Boy Scouts said, "We intentionally developed an open, accessible process to reach survivors and help them take an essential step toward receiving compensation. The response we have seen from survivors has been gut wrenching. We are deeply sorry."

With enrollment plummeting and sponsors dropping out, the future of the organization remains tenuous.[6]

ACKNOWLEDGMENTS

I am overwhelmed with the blessings that brought me through to the good after passing through the bad and the ugly. Without these trials in my life, I wouldn't be fit to help others who have gone through the same. Without the Lord, I wouldn't be here at all. I am full of utter thankfulness to be able to share my heart through this book.

Redemption is happening all over the place through the vision of a pastor and his wife. Thank you so much, Pastor Ross Holtz, for all your support over the years and for sharing breakfast with me that morning, which led to the idea of writing a book in the first place. Thank you, Athena Dean Holtz and Redemption Press, for embracing my story and going with it.

A special thanks to my content editor and rewriter, Sarah Barnum, for reworking my story into its current form. Your knowledge, wisdom, and patience helped tell my story in the best way possible.

Thank you, Pastor Marcus Kelly, for your friendship and support, especially regarding taking on the hard stuff with the death of my son. I appreciate your moral support through my toughest moments more than words can express.

Thank you, Pastor James Ludlow, for always believing in me and my life story.

I am forever grateful to Rene Stam and her mother, Delphine, for going through my Boy Scout memorabilia. My story would have never been told without this act of love.

Thank you, Zane and Julie Thompson, for all your love and support along the way, including hearing my life story at the Seattle and Portland Salvation Army Rehab Centers.

Thanks, Portillo family, for your love, friendship, and humor throughout this journey.

Thanks, Dean Smith of Live to Forgive Ministries. You have given me confidence like no other. Thank you for your humor and your wisdom to help me and so many others.

My heartfelt appreciation also goes to my brother, Matt. Without you, I would still be stuck in the shoving-it-down-deep mode. Your boldness enabled me to arrive at knowing what it really means to forgive. You saved my life, Matt.

Finally, I thank God every moment for my beautiful children, Brian and Becca. God has really carried us through the furnace of losing Benny. I couldn't be prouder of you both. I love you more than you will ever know.

NOTES

1. The percentage of Scouts achieving Eagle Scout was 2 percent in the 1970s. In 2019 it was 8 percent, per http://www. scouting.org/wp-content/uploads/2020/03/2019-Eagle-Scouts-Formatted.pdf.

2. Laura Lambert, "Stockholm Syndrome," *Britannica*, accessed June 2, 2021, https://www.britannica.com/science/ Stockholm-syndrome.

3. https://www.nytimes.com/1935/05/18/archives/boy-scouts-red-flag-list-bars-undesirables-col-roosevelt-says-we.html.

4. https://en.wikipedia.org/wiki/Boy_Scouts_of_America_sex_ abuse_cases#cite_note-ScoutsHonor-4.

5. Patrick Boyle, *Scout's Honor: Sexual Abuse in America's Most Trusted Institution* (Prima Publishing, 1994).

6. At least 92,000 have filed sex abuse claims against the Boy Scouts, legal team says," CNN, accessed April 14, 2021, https:// www.cnn.com/2020/11/16/us/boy-scouts-sex-abuse-deadline-bankruptcy/index.html.

ORDER INFORMATION

To order additional copies of this book, please visit
www.redemption-press.com.
Also available on Amazon.com and BarnesandNoble.com
or by calling toll-free 1-844-2REDEEM.